The Prose of the World

Maurice Merleau-Ponty

Edited by

Translated by

The Prose of the World

Claude Lefort
John O'Neill

HEINEMANN · LONDON

Heinemann Educational Books Ltd

LONDON EDINBURGH MELBOURNE AUCKLAND
TORONTO HONG KONG SINGAPORE
KUALA LUMPUR IBADAN NAIROBI
JOHANNESBURG NEW DELHI

ISBN 0 435 82688 3

First published in this edition 1974

Originally published in French under the title
La Prose du monde

This volume is published in a uniform edition together with *Adventures of the Dialectic* and a selection, edited by John O'Neill, entitled *Phenomenology, Language and Sociology*. This selection is taken from *Signs, Sense and Non-Sense* and *The Primacy of Perception*. John O'Neill's monograph on Merleau-Ponty, *Perception, Expression and History*, forms an introduction to the volume

Published by Heinemann Educational Books Ltd
48 Charles Street, London W1X 8AH

Printed in Great Britain by
Fletcher & Son Ltd, Norwich

Contents

Editor's Preface

THE WORK which Maurice Merleau-Ponty planned to call *The Prose of the World,* or *Introduction to the Prose of the World,* is unfinished. There is good reason to believe that the author deliberately abandoned it and that, had he lived, he would not have completed it, at least in the form that he first outlined.

Once finished, the book was to constitute the first section of a two-part work—the second would have had a more distinctly metaphysical nature—whose aim was to offer us, as an extension of the *Phenomenology of Perception,* a theory of truth. We have evidence of the underlying plan of this work, the more precious because the notes or outlines that we found are of little help, in Merleau-Ponty's report to Professor Martial Gueroult when he was a candidate for admission to the Collège de France.[1] In this document Merleau-Ponty sets out the principal ideas of his early publications and indicates that, since 1945, he has been engaged in new research

> which will definitively fix the philosophical significance of my earlier works while they, in turn, determine the route and the method of these later studies.
>
> I found in the experience of the perceived world a new type of

1. "An Unpublished Text by Maurice Merleau-Ponty: A Prospectus of His Work," trans. Arleen B. Dallery, in *The Primacy of Perception,* ed. James M. Edie (Evanston: Northwestern University Press, 1964).

relation between the mind and truth. The evidence of the perceived thing lies in its concrete aspect, in the very texture of its qualities, and in the equivalence among all its sensible properties—which caused Cézanne to say that one should be able to paint even odors. Before our undivided existence the world is true; it exists. The unity, the articulations of both are intermingled. We experience in it a truth which shows through and envelops us rather than being held and circumscribed by our mind.

Now if we consider, above the perceived world, the field of knowledge properly so called—i.e., the field in which the mind seeks to possess the truth, to define its objects itself, and thus to attain to a universal wisdom, not tied to the particularities of our situation—we must ask: Does not the realm of the perceived world take on the form of a simple appearance? Is not pure understanding a new source of knowledge, in comparison with which our perceptual familiarity with the world is only a rough, unformed sketch? We are obliged to answer these questions first with a theory of truth and then with a theory of intersubjectivity, both of which I have already touched upon in essays such as "Le Doute de Cézanne" [Cézanne's Doubt] "Le Roman et la métaphysique" [Metaphysics and the Novel],[2] and, on the philosophy of history, in *Humanisme et terreur* (1947) [Humanism and Terror].[3] But the philosophical foundations of these essays are still to be rigorously elaborated. I am now working on two books dealing with a theory of truth.[4]

These two books are named a little further on: "The Origin of Truth" and "Introduction to the Prose of the World." Merleau-Ponty defines their common purpose as to found, upon the discovery of the body as active body or symbolic power, "a concrete theory of the mind which will show the mind in a relationship of reciprocal exchange with the instruments which it uses." [5] To refrain from any commentary which could mislead the reader, we limit ourselves to pointing out that the concrete theory of mind was to be constructed around a new idea of expression which was yet to be completed, of an analysis of gestures or the mimetic

2. TRANSLATOR: These are the first two essays in *Sense and Non-Sense*, trans. Hubert L. Dreyfus and Patricia A. Dreyfus (Evanston: Northwestern University Press, 1964), pp. 9–40.

3. *Humanism and Terror: An Essay on the Communist Problem*, trans. John O'Neill (Boston: Beacon Press, 1969).

4. TRANSLATOR: "An Unpublished Text," pp. 6–7.

5. TRANSLATOR: *Ibid.*

uses of the body and of all forms of language, to the most sublimated language of mathematics. However, we should draw attention to a few lines which clarify the outline of *The Prose of the World* and refer to the finished work.

> Since I intend to treat this problem more fully in my work *L'Origine de la vérité* [The Origin of Truth], I have approached it less directly in a partially written book dealing with literary language. In this area it is easier to show that language is never the mere clothing of a thought which otherwise possesses itself in full clarity. The meaning of a book is given, in the first instance, not so much by its ideas as by a systematic and unexpected variation of the modes of language, of narrative, or of existing literary forms. This accent, this particular modulation of speech—if the expression is successful—is assimilated little by little by the reader, and it gives him access to a thought to which he was until then indifferent or even opposed. Communication in literature is not the simple appeal on the part of the writer to meanings which would be part of an *a priori* of the mind; rather, communication arouses these meanings in the mind through enticement and a kind of oblique action. The writer's thought does not control his language from without; the writer is himself a kind of new idiom, constructing itself, inventing ways of expression, and diversifying itself according to its own meaning. Perhaps poetry is only that part of literature where this autonomy is ostentatiously displayed. All great prose is also a re-creation of the signifying instrument, henceforth manipulated according to a new syntax. Prosaic writing, on the other hand, limits itself to using, through accepted signs, the meanings already accepted in a given culture. Great prose is the art of capturing a meaning which until then had never been objectified and of rendering it accessible to everyone who speaks the same language. When a writer is no longer capable of thus founding a new universality and of taking the risk of communicating, he has outlived his time. It seems to me that we can also say of other institutions that they have ceased to live when they show themselves incapable of carrying on a poetry of human relations—that is, the call of each individual freedom to all the others.
>
> Hegel said that the Roman state was the prose of the world. I shall entitle my book *Introduction à la prose du monde* [Introduction to the Prose of the World]. In this work I shall elaborate the category of prose beyond the confines of literature to give it a sociological meaning.[6]

6. TRANSLATOR: *Ibid.*, pp. 8–9.

Merleau-Ponty's account is definitely the best presentation of *The Prose of the World.* It also has the merit of throwing some light on the date of the work's composition. Addressed to Professor Gueroult shortly before Merleau-Ponty's appointment to the Collège de France in February, 1952, it undoubtedly refers to the 170 pages found among Merleau-Ponty's papers after his death. These must be the pages that make up the first half of the book then interrupted. This opinion is based upon two complementary observations. The first is that in August, 1952, Merleau-Ponty made a note which contains an inventory of the themes already treated, and this note, although brief, clearly designates the group of chapters that we possess. The second is that, between the time when he informed Professor Gueroult of the state of progress of his work and August, Merleau-Ponty decided to extract from *The Prose of the World* an important chapter, considerably modified, for publication as an essay in *Les Temps modernes*. The essay appeared in June and July of the same year as "Indirect Language and the Voices of Silence." [7] However, we have proof that this essay was not undertaken before March: its opening refers to a book by Pierre Francastel, *Peinture et société,* published in February. Of course, these few elements do not enable us to fix the exact date at which the manuscript was interrupted. Nevertheless, they authorize us to think it was certainly not later than the beginning of 1952, perhaps a few months earlier. But since we know, from a letter Merleau-Ponty wrote to his wife the previous summer, that he was devoting most of his work during the holidays to *The Prose of the World,* it is legitimate to suppose that the halt came in the autumn of 1951 or, at the latest, the beginning of that winter.

On the other hand, there are less precise indications of the beginning of *The Prose of the World.* The third chapter—whose object is to compare pictorial language with literary language—could not have begun before the publication of the last volume of Malraux's *Psychologie de l'art,* that is, before July, 1950: the references to the "currency of the Absolute" leave no doubt on this

7. TRANSLATOR: Published in *Signs,* trans. Richard C. McCleary (Evanston: Northwestern University Press, 1964), pp. 39–83.

point. A consideration of Merleau-Ponty's study of André Malraux, part of which we found in a long summary *cum* commentary, inclines us to believe that they are separated by only a few weeks or months. Moreover, we should note that during this period Merleau-Ponty was teaching at the Sorbonne and also devoting part of his time to *Les Temps modernes*.[8] Our hypothesis is strengthened by the presence of several references to an article by Maurice Blanchot. "Le Musée, l'art et le temps," published in *Critique*, December, 1950. These references return us to 1951.

Nothing prevents us, of course, from supposing that the first two chapters were almost finished when Merleau-Ponty decided to buttress his argument with Malraux's analysis. Some such change in the course of his work seems likely. However, we doubt that it occurred, since all the outlines we have found contain a chapter on language and painting, and the state of the manuscript suggests no break in its composition. It is also significant that the example of the painter is taken up in the last pages of the second chapter, prior to proceeding in strict logic to the middle of the third chapter. Thus we are inclined to conclude that Merleau-Ponty wrote the first half of *The Prose of the World* in the space of one year.

But it is certain that he had the idea of a book on language—more precisely, on literature—much earlier. If Malraux's work influenced his enterprise, Sartre's *What Is Literature?*, appearing in 1947, made a profound impression on Merleau-Ponty and

8. TRANSLATOR: Merleau-Ponty held the chair of psychology and pedagogy at the Sorbonne from 1949 to 1952. *The Prose of the World* contains material from his courses, "La Méthode en psychologie de l'enfant" and "La Conscience et l'acquisition du langage." These courses, reconstructed from student notes with Merleau-Ponty's approval, were eventually published as articles in *Bulletin de psychologie*, XVIII, no. 236 (November, 1964), 109–40, 226–59. The latter article, translated by Hugh J. Silverman as *Consciousness and the Acquisition of Language*, is forthcoming from Northwestern University Press. André Robinet refers to Merleau-Ponty's teaching a course on general psychology and aesthetics at the University of Lyon in 1947–48 and one entitled "General Psychology: Language and Communication" there in 1948–49 (Robinet, *Merleau-Ponty, sa vie, son oeuvre, avec un exposé de sa philosophie* [Paris: Presses Universitaires de France, 1963], p. 69).

confirmed his intention to treat the problems of expression. He wrote a substantial résumé of Sartre's essay in 1948 or 1949—probably after the publication in May, 1948, of *Situations II*, from which all the references are taken—and accompanied it with a critical commentary which occasionally shows a vigorous opposition to Sartre's theses; Numerous ideas which are the burden of *The Prose of the World* were enounced here and related to a work in progress. However, the latter had not received a precise form. At this period Merleau-Ponty adopted the notion of prose in its purely literary use; he had found neither the title nor the genuine theme of his future book. Thus he settled for noting at the end of his commentary: "I must do a sort of *What Is Literature?* with a longer section on the sign and prose, not a whole dialectic of literature, but five literary studies: Montaigne, Stendhal, Proust, Breton, Artaud." An undated note, but already mentioning the title *The Prose of the World*, suggests that he imagined a much larger work, in several volumes, whose aim would be to apply the redefined categories of prose and poetry to the accounts of literature, love, religion, and politics. There is no discussion of the works of the linguists which later have an important place. More significant, there is no mention of any study of painting. His silence on this point allows us to assume that, at this date, he had not read the *Psychologie de l'art* or estimated how much he could draw upon it for a theory of expression. Moreover, we should not infer that Merleau-Ponty's interest in linguistics or painting had not yet been awakened. He had already examined the work of Saussure and Vendryès, using them notably in his commentary on *What Is Literature?* His essay on "Cézanne's Doubt," published in *Fontaine* in 1945 (reprinted in *Sense and Non-Sense*) but written several years before, and courses at the University of Lyon, are further testimony to the role that reflection on pictorial expression played in his research. At the most, we can submit that, in the first sketch of *The Prose of the World*, he did not think of making use of this reflection and did so only in 1950 or 1951, once he had decided to limit his work more strictly.

We can only propose a hypothesis about the reasons for this decision. On the basis of part of the letter to Professor Gueroult, we can say that the idea of writing another book, "The Origin of Truth," which would reveal the metaphysical meaning of Merleau-Ponty's theory of expression, could have led him to modify and to reduce his original project. To do so, he would have had to proceed to relate—as in fact he does—the problems of the systematic nature of language and of its historicity, to relate the problems of artistic creation and scientific knowledge, and finally, to relate the problems of expression and of truth. Did it not become necessary simultaneously to subordinate what he first had conceived as a preliminary work to the fundamental task that he now discerned? In brief, we believe that the last conception of *The Prose of the World* is the index of a new stage of Merleau-Ponty's thought. When he begins to write this book, he is preoccupied with another project which does not cancel the one in progress but limits its breadth.

If we are correct, we may be better prepared to answer other more pressing questions. Why did Merleau-Ponty interrupt his work in 1952, when he was already halfway through it? Does this interruption constitute an abandonment or a disavowal?

There are signs that the philosopher remained attached to his enterprise for a long time. At the Collège de France, he chose as the subjects of his first two courses, in 1953–54, "The Sensible World and Expression" and "The Literary Use of Language." [9] The second theme, in particular, gave him the opportunity to discuss Stendhal and Valéry, whom, according to notes, he intended to treat in his book. In the following year, he again considers "The Problem of Speech." [10] However, apart from his teaching he was working in another direction. He reread Marx, Lenin, and Trotsky and accumulated considerable notes on Weber and Lukács which were part of his next project, *Les Aventures de la dialectique*, published in 1955.[11] Nothing indicates that by this time he had abandoned *The Prose of the World.* On the contrary, a note, "revision of the manuscript" (difficult, however, to in-

9. *Themes from the Lectures at the Collège de France, 1952–1960*, trans. John O'Neill (Evanston: Northwestern University Press, 1970).

10. *Ibid.*

11. TRANSLATOR: See "Materials for a Theory of History," in *Themes from the Lectures*, and *Adventures of the Dialectic*, trans. Joseph Bien (London: Heinemann Educational Books, 1974).

terpret, because it seems to mix, with the résumé of the text written so far, new formulations which perhaps contain important modifications) persuades us that, through its reference to a course given in 1954–55, Merleau-Ponty is still interested in the project, at least four years after composing the first chapters.[12] But for how long is he interested? In the absence of any dated findings, we can only hazard a hypothesis. Before 1959, several rough drafts trace the outline of another work with the title, "Being and the World," or "Genealogy of Truth," or the one already known, "The Origin of Truth." Finally, "Indirect Language and the Voices of Silence" in 1959 seems to take the place of the work laid aside.

But to suppose that the abandonment was final in no way implies any condemnation of the work actually done. It is more probable that the reasons which, in 1951 or a little earlier, led him to reduce the proportions of the work later prevented Merleau-Ponty from resuming the interrupted manuscript. His first desire, to write a new "What Is Literature?" and through this to rejoin the general problem of expression and institution, was definitely precluded by the wish to write a new "What Is Metaphysics?" This task did not make the old enterprise useless but prevented him from returning to it. It undoubtedly occupied him increasingly until it was embodied in *The Visible and the Invisible,* which in 1959 took the place of "The Origin of Truth." [13]

However, we are not satisfied with an appeal to psychological motives to understand the change of emphasis between the works. We feel that it was the result of a profound overhaul of the problematic elaborated in the early theses. If we consult the report to Professor Gueroult, or the qualifications and works listed in support of his candidacy at the Collège de France, we see that at that time Merleau-Ponty persistently emphasizes the continuity between his early and more recent studies. If we then consider the notes to the text of *The Visible and the Invisible,* we

12. TRANSLATOR: "Institution in Personal and Public History," in *Themes from the Lectures.*

13. TRANSLATOR: *The Visible and the Invisible,* ed. Claude Lefort, trans. Alphonso Lingis (Evanston: Northwestern University Press, 1968).

must conclude that he is submitting the perspective adopted in the *Phenomenology of Perception* to a radical critique. From 1952 to 1959 a new task imposes itself, and his language is transformed. He discovers the delusions in which "philosophies of consciousness" are trapped and from which his own critique of classical metaphysics has not saved him. He begins to confront the necessity of providing an ontological foundation for the analyses of the body and perception that had been his starting point. It is not enough to say that he turns toward metaphysics and that this intention separates him from *The Prose of the World.* The movement which carries him toward a new book is both more violent and more faithful to the early inspiration, so that we can imagine it only by considering the genres from which the two works seem to originate. The truth is that, in Merleau-Ponty's last years, metaphysics no longer appeared to him to be the ground of all his thoughts. He allowed himself to be carried beyond its frontiers and entertained an interrogation of being which shattered the former status of the subject and of truth. Thus, in a sense, he went far beyond the positions outlined in the documents of 1952. In addition, the underlying thought in *The Visible and the Invisible* germinates in the first sketch of *The Prose of the World;* it then experiences a series of changes that culminate in the interruption of the manuscript—but in such a way that the impossibility of pursuing the earlier work, instead of being the result of a new choice, is rather its fulfillment.

To be sure, we are not forgetting the terms of the communication to Professor Gueroult. In 1952, Merleau-Ponty judged that *The Structure of Behavior* and the *Phenomenology of Perception* provided the "itinerary" and "method" of his new studies. However, the report is only a sketch, which, as Merleau-Ponty himself has taught us, must be confronted with experience, that is, with the language of the work under way, with the effective powers of prose. Now, a reader familiar with Merleau-Ponty's last writings will not agree with him entirely. He will see, in *The Prose of the World,* a new conception appear of man's relation with history and with truth; he will discover, in the meditation on "indirect language," the first signs of the "indirect ontology" which sustains *The Visible and the Invisible*. If he rereads the notes of the latter, moreover, he will see that the questions raised in the earlier manuscript are reformulated in many places and in similar terms, and—whether involving language, structure, history, or literary creation—are intended to be included in the work in progress. We therefore unhesitatingly respond negatively to the question, does the abandonment of the manuscript constitute a disavowal? The very term "abandonment" seems to us equivocal. "Abandonment" implies that Merleau-Ponty would never have returned to the work he had started with the sole intention of giving it a finish that it lacked. On the other hand, it must be admitted that *The Prose of the World,* down to the very literalness of certain analyses, could have been reborn in the tissue of *The Visible and the Invisible,* if the latter had not itself been interrupted by the philosopher's death.

It remains for us to say that this text, published through our efforts, would not have come from its author. We are presenting it as the first half of a book whose second part is unlikely to have been written—if it had been written, it would have provoked such a profound modification of the earlier part that we would have had another work. Since the information we have given does not make it superfluous, but, on the contrary, demands that the editor justify his undertaking, let us add that there are other objections to this publication. For the third chapter of *The Prose of the World* had already appeared in a similar version, while the manuscript reveals negligence, especially repetitions which Merleau-Ponty would never have let pass in a final version. We formulated these objections a long time ago but did not think them overwhelming. Perhaps it is a risk to give the public a manuscript set aside by its author; but how much more serious the decision to put it back into the trunk from which his own people had taken it, when we ourselves have found it supplies a greater ability to understand Merleau-Ponty's work and to examine the thought he left us. What a loss we would inflict upon readers who, now more than when he wrote, are very interested in the problems of language, by depriving them of a light that one hardly sees shed elsewhere. Finally, what conventions should one follow which would prevail over the demands of philosophical knowledge, and before which one should submit himself when the only one who could relate us has been silenced, These reflections were enough for us: Merleau-Ponty says in *The Prose of the World* that which he has not said in his other books. He would undoubtedly have resumed and developed it in *The Visible and the Invisible,* but even there it did not reach expression. To be sure, the reader will observe that a part of the text is similar to "Indirect Language and the Voices of Silence." However, if he is careful he will also measure the differences and gain an added interest from the comparison. Of course, he cannot fail to notice the faults of composition, but he would indeed be unjust not to agree that Merleau-Ponty, even when he manages to be less than his best, remains an incomparable guide.

CLAUDE LEFORT

Editorial Note

THE TEXT OF *The Prose of the World*, as we have pointed out, consists of 170 loose-leaf, typewritten pages, for the most part covered on only one side. A certain number of pages contain abundant corrections. Hardly any pages have no corrections. Neither the title of the work nor its date is mentioned.

The manuscript comprises four parts expressly indicated by roman numerals, on pages 1, 8, 53, and 127. We have distinguished two other parts by the internal logic of the work's composition: a fifth, beginning on page 145, because there is an unusually large space at the head of the page; and a sixth, on page 163, suggested by a sign (a cross in a triangle) and an analogous large space at the top of the page. The order adopted corresponds to the directions in the note of August, 1952 (entitled "revision of the manuscript"), which contains six paragraphs, of which only the first four are actually numbered.

We thought it well to give titles to the six chapters thus constituted, since Merleau-Ponty does not provide any. Their only function is to designate as clearly as possible the principal theme of the argument. The terms we have used are borrowed from the text.

We cannot publish the notes, or outlines, we have found, because they are undated, occasionally confused or very elliptic, and discordant. Also, it was impossible to select some among them without involving an interpretation which would rightly seem arbitrary. All that we can say is that they suggest a second part that would have been devoted to a study of some literary selections—most often from Stendhal, Proust, Valéry, Breton, and Artaud—and a third part that would have considered the problem of the prose of the world in its generality, but with special attention to politics and religion.

Instead, we have reproduced Merleau-Ponty's notes in the margin of the text or at the bottom of the page. These will perhaps disappoint many readers, as their formulation is so condensed or abrupt. Such readers may ignore them without any difficulty; others will benefit from these notes.

In transcribing, we have made it a rule to limit our own intervention most severely. When we found an insignificant error (an unwarranted change of gender or number), we have corrected it; whenever the correction called for the substitution of words, we have used *sic* to draw the reader's attention to it. Wherever possible, we have given more precise or more complete references.

Finally, the notes, whether they are the editor's, the translator's, or Merleau-Ponty's, are numbered consecutively in each chapter; notes by the editor and translator are identified to differentiate them from Merleau-Ponty's. The author's marginal notes are indicated by an asterisk.

The convention adopted to indicate words that could not be read is as follows:

illegible: [?]

doubtful but probable: [subject?]

Translator's Introduction: Language and the Voice of Philosophy

WE CANNOT BEGIN Merleau-Ponty's text by missing the significance of an *introduction*, for that would be precisely to fall into the prose of the world which any beginning makes thematic. Therefore I shall not concern myself with a conventional version of the place of *The Prose of the World* among Merleau-Ponty's other writings.[1] We may count upon others to do this with possibly even more patience and forbearance than are exercised in Claude Lefort's editorial remarks.[2] Avoiding such textual concerns may

1. Merleau-Ponty's note on the philosophy of speech and the malaise of culture is what I have in mind as a comment on much conventional philosophical work. "There is a danger that a philosophy of speech would justify the indefinite proliferation of writings—and even of pre-writings (working notes—Husserl's *Forschungsmanuskript.* With him notion of the *Arbeitsprobleme——Arbeit:* that impossible enterprise of grasping the transcendental consciousness in the act)—the habit of speaking without knowing what one is saying, the confusion of style and thought etc.

Yet: 1) it has always been that way in fact—the works that escape this profusion are '*academic*' works

2) there is a remedy, which is not to return to the American analytic-academic method—which would be to retreat from the problem—but to proceed over and beyond by facing the things again" (*The Visible and the Invisible*, ed. Claude Lefort, trans. Alphonso Lingis [Evanston: Northwestern University Press, 1968], p. 239).

2. Those who take the notion of philosophical work seriously will have to build upon what has already been achieved in the following careful analyses: James M. Edie, "Can Grammar Be Thought?," in *Patterns of the Life-World: Essays in Honor of John Wild,* ed.

seem, however, to deprive my own introductory effort of any place. Of course, it does not, because its value must consist in *underlying* the text, coming neither before nor after it. In other words, an introduction must seem to be necessary to what is around it. To break the linearity of its text, to be more than figurative, an introduction must respond to its topic. For it is its character as a response that determines the authenticity of an introduction as a way to the text or from the text to its horizons.

Phenomenology is remarkable for its introductions not only of itself but also of the world to which it returns us. Here we need a beginning which will catch [3] or fetch out a sense of Merleau-Ponty's conception of the relation between language and the world and simultaneously convey this preoccupation as an expression of the crisis in philosophy in the same manner that Husserl considered that concern to be an authentic introduction to phenomenology. Such a beginning seems necessary because I see in Merleau-Ponty's work, from beginning to end, a critique of the two principal techniques of reason, namely, the analytic method of experimental science and the structuralist method of the human sciences through which the tradition of rationalism dominates the world by removing the responsible subject of human history. The success of Western science and its industrial organization is, as Weber and Marx showed, the result of an asceticism at the roots of the positivist mode of rationality. The methodological and technical success of Western science rests, as

---

James M. Edie, Francis H. Parker, and Calvin O. Schrag (Evanston: Northwestern University Press, 1970), pp. 315–45; James M. Edie, "Was Merleau-Ponty a Structuralist?," *Semiotica* (1972), pp. 297–323; Maurice Lagueux, "Merleau-Ponty et la linguistique de Saussure: Dialogue," *Canadian Philosophical Review,* IV, no. 3 (1965), 351–64. "Was Merleau-Ponty a Structuralist?," in particular, furnishes the basic data as well as raising the fundamental questions which may guide further research in Merleau-Ponty's phenomenology of language. My own approach is determined by an interest in the way the phenomenology of language furnishes a key to similar analyses of cultural institutions in general.

3. For a phenomenology of the notion of "catch" and the related experience and concept of "surrender," see Kurt H. Wolff, *Surrender and Catch: A Palimpsest Story,* Sorokin Memorial Lecture, No. 3 (Saskatoon: University of Saskatchewan Press, 1972).

Husserl observes, upon a *residual concept* of reason which excludes any treatment of the *problems of reason.*[4] But these observations form part of the self-criticism of the ideal of phenomenology as a rigorous science begun by Husserl himself and, as I believe, adopted as the working principle of Merleau-Ponty's own phenomenology.

The problematic of *The Prose of the World* has been outlined in Merleau-Ponty's interpretation of the main features of Husserlian phenomenology—for example, in his remarks on the notions of essence and eidetic reduction.

> Every reduction, says Husserl, as well as being transcendental is necessarily eidetic. That means that we cannot subject our perception of the world to philosophical scrutiny without ceasing to be identified with that act of positing the world, with that interest in it which delimits us, without drawing back from our commitment which is itself thus made to appear as a spectacle, without passing from the *fact* of our existence to its *nature,* from the Dasein to the Wesen. But it is clear that the essence is here not the end, but a means, that our effective involvement in the world is precisely what has to be understood and made amenable to conceptualization, for it is what polarizes all our conceptual particularizations. . . . Whatever the subtle changes of meaning which have ultimately brought us, as a linguistic acquisition, the word and concept of consciousness, we enjoy direct access to what it designates. For we have the experience of ourselves, of that consciousness which we are, and it is on the basis of this experience that all linguistic connotations are assessed, and precisely through it that language comes to have any meaning at all for us. "It is that as yet dumb experience . . . which we are concerned to lead to the pure expression of its own meaning." Husserl's essences are destined to bring back all the living relationships of experience, as the fisherman's net draws up from the depths of the ocean quivering fish and seaweed.[5]

4. Edmund Husserl, *The Crisis of European Sciences and Transcendental Phenomenology: An Introduction to Phenomenological Philosophy,* trans. David Carr (Evanston: Northwestern University Press, 1970), p. 9.

5. Maurice Merleau-Ponty, *Phenomenology of Perception,* trans. Colin Smith (London: Routledge & Kegan Paul; New York: Humanities Press, 1965), pp. xiv–xv. The internal quotation is from Husserl, *Méditations Cartésiennes*, trans. Gabrielle Peiffer and Emmanuel Levinas (Paris: Colin, 1931), p. 33.

Merleau-Ponty's formulation of the return to phenomena is not intended to do away with language as such but to recover from its particular vocabularies the genesis of the world and its appearance, that is the inspiration of poetry or of any creative act. Indeed, so far from being destructive of philosophical language and its intentionality, Merleau-Ponty's appeal to the prelinguistic world is an effort to free philosophical thinking from the habits of method and to reconnect it with the teleology of reason.

> Through this broadened notion of intentionality, phenomenological "comprehension" is distinguished from traditional "intellection," which is confined to "true and immutable natures," and so phenomenology can become a phenomenology of origins. Whether we are concerned with a thing perceived, a historical event or a doctrine, to "understand" is to take in the total intention—not only what these things are for representation (the "properties" of the thing perceived, the mass of "historical facts," the "ideas" introduced by the doctrine)—but the unique mode of existing expressed in the properties of the pebble, the glass or the piece of wax, in all the events of a revolution, in all the thoughts of a philosopher. It is a matter, in the case of each civilization, of finding the Idea in the Hegelian sense, that is, not a law of the physico-mathematical type, discoverable by objective thought, but that formula which sums up some unique manner of behaviour towards others, towards Nature, time and death: a certain way of patterning the world which the historian should be capable of seizing upon and making his own. These are the *dimensions* of history.[6]

These remarks of Merleau-Ponty are clearly programatic, but there are many senses in which this may be understood. I wish to choose the direction of his concluding remarks upon phenomenological method as a way of moving further along the path which Merleau-Ponty himself opened into the tradition of reason in the human world.

> Probably the chief gain from phenomenology is to have united extreme subjectivism and extreme objectivism in its notion of the world or of rationality. Rationality is precisely measured by the experiences in which it is disclosed. To say that there exists rationality is to say that perspectives blend, perceptions confirm

6. *Phenomenology of Perception*, p. xviii.

> each other, a meaning emerges. But it should not be set in a realm apart, transposed into absolute Spirit, or into a world in the realist sense. The phenomenological world is not pure being, but the sense which is revealed where the paths of my various experiences intersect, and also where my own and other people's intersect and engage each other like gears. It is thus inseparable from subjectivity and intersubjectivity, which find their unity when I either take up my past experiences in those of the present, or other people's in my own.[7]

The relation between speaking and the structure of language raises the question of the dependence of the word on its divine anchorage, on ourselves and the variety of human history and culture. The responsibility of speech marks the autonomy of philosophical reflection amidst sophistry and rhetoric. But our own care with language belongs to the responsibility we have to ourselves and to the nature of things. This, however, is not an invocation of a science of language in its present sense or, in particular, its subordination of common sense everyday language. It is an invocation of the common labor of turning common sense into good sense. That is, it is an idealization of the community of truth rather than the packaging of being into competing domains of knowledge ruled by definitions and operations.

There are, of course, as many philosophies as there are philosophies of language. It has thus seemed to many that language is the scandal of philosophy, that a rigorous philosophy can be achieved only through the adoption of a "mathematical" language. The republic of knowledge is in this way made the construct of a rule of method which would provide future natives with greater clarity of judgment than philosophers of the past. This Cartesian dream of a universal language is at the same time, therefore, a prescription for social order, since clarity of mind eliminates the vexatiousness of theological and political controversy—not to mention the vanity of poets. The standards of science and technology translate the ideals of philosophical enlightenment and community into the everyday practices of public knowledge, health, and security. Plain language becomes the order of the day. Metaphysics and feudal privilege are swept into

7. *Ibid.*, pp. xix–xx.

the trash of history. The new society is uniform and its icon is a "well-made language," the sublimation of civic order and technical optimism.

The pathos of philosophical speech is romantic and historicist. It rejects the universalism of scientific language in search of human expression and its power to say man through the structures of divinity, stone and commerce. A philosophy of speech is properly a philosophy of initiative, of style and gratuity accomplished against the limits of received language. Speech is the invocation of our own being in concert with others. This is so even when our speech is disordered or mere chatter. The commonality of language and being is the prepredicative source of all predicative orders or domains of being and togetherness, as well as of alienation and falsehood. The efficacy of speech may present itself to us as the workings of an external order, of magic and institution, of divine fiat or plain sense. But these are equally the responses of speech in which nature, language, and society are addressed as the other of dialogue. We never escape the antinomy of expression and communication, because meaning is neither a collective representation nor a solitary accomplishment. The options of madness and officialese are the result of the suppression of the complementary orders of speech and communication. The expropriation of meaning is as pervasive in modern times as the alienation of labor. Its cause cannot without contradiction be attributed to language, art, and work. For each of these is the irremediable means of complaint and reform. What is expropriated is the standard by which we have anything in common.

> When both of us see what you say is true, when we both see what I say is true—where do we see it, I ask you? Certainly, it is not in you that I see it, it is not in me that you see it. Both of us see it in immutable Truth, which is beyond our minds. [Augustine *Confessions* XII 35]

All agreements of fact are thus agreements in principle, that is, agreements of value which ground rules of logic and the common verbal and artistic currency. The crisis of communication is a crisis of transcendental values. Thus the modern concern with love, friendship, and communication is a concern about the fate of consciousness, of our being with being, that is, the hospitality of being.

The poet's experience with language and the artist's relation to tradition and style always appealed to Merleau-Ponty as the ground for the relation between expression and communication. Here we are tempted to speak of mastery and technique and to overlook the fact that these are only so many ways of being-in-the-world through our senses, through perception, language, and art. The science of language, as well as the history of philosophy and the history of art and science, begin with an autonomous object of study. But the life of philosophy, science, and the arts acquires its autonomy only through the subscription of living thinkers and artists whose encounter with tradition and its solicitation of their responses require that their own lives be the material and setting of the artifacts they create. The acquisition of speech, of thought, and of style is not a trick of skill, of technique, or of method.

The Prose of the World presupposes and illustrates Merleau-Ponty's conceptions of intersubjectivity and rationality and the fundamentals of his philosophy of perception and embodiment.[8] The phenomenological approach to language is ultimately an introduction to the ontology of the world. It is a reflection upon our being-in-the world through embodiment, which is the mysterious action of a presence that can be elsewhere. The philosophical puzzles of how we are in the world (ontology) or of how the world can be in us (epistemology), which have dictated quite particular analyses of the logic of language and thought, are transcended in the phenomenological conception of embodiment as a corporeal intentionality, a mode of knowledge and expressive form.

I reach for my pen when I am ready to write, without consciously thematizing the pen as something with which to write or the distance between myself and where the pen lies. My hand is already looking for something with which to write and, as it

8. John O'Neill, *Perception, Expression, and History: The Social Phenomenology of Maurice Merleau-Ponty* (Evanston: Northwestern University Press, 1970).

were, scans the desk for a pen or pencil which is there "somewhere," where it usually is or where I have just put it down, so that it too seems to guide my hand in its search. But I can look for the pen only because in some sense I have my hand on it. If writing were painful to me or if I were sensible of having to write to someone for whom I did not care or I had only bad news, I could "put off" writing because I did not "feel" like writing. My pen there on the desk would not invite me to pick it up except with a painful reminder of my relations with someone else. Thus the structure of the experience of writing is there in my fingers, in the pen, and in my relations to the person to whom I am writing. It is neither a structure which I "represent" to myself —which would not take into account the knowledge in my fingers—nor is it a simple "reflex" stimulated by my pen—which would overlook my relations to the person to whom I am writing. The structure of writing is an "ensemble" in which the elements function only together and whose expressive value for me plays upon my relation to myself and others.

In the same way, speech is a capacity I acquire for communication. It arises not just from the expressive values of the words when joined with due respect for logic and syntax but also from my experience of the world, other persons, and the language I inhabit. Linguistics as a science of language treats language as a natural object, and logic treats it as an entirely artificial object. The linguistic conception of language presents language as a universe from which man is absent and with him the consequences of time and the disclosure of nature in magic, myth, and poetry. In logic man's power over language, which is ignored in linguistics, is raised above magic and poetry to the creation of a *mathesis universalis* which sloughs off all historical languages and purifies the word once and for all. The linguistic conception of the relation of language to meaning breaks down for the very reason that a language tells us nothing except about itself.[9] The problems of discrimination, quantification, and predictability that concern the statistical treatment of language are independent

9. On the relations among language, logic, linguistics, and semantics, see Mikel Dufrenne, *Language and Philosophy*, trans. Henry B. Veatch (Bloomington: Indiana University Press, 1963).

of the semantic value of the information being processed. It is words and not phonemes which carry meaning. Furthermore, words have meaning on their own account, especially such words as "liberty" or "love," but also as elements in a whole which is not just the phrase or sentence but the entire "mother" language. To know the meaning of a word is not just a question of acquiring an appropriate phonetic motivation. It involves a familiarity with an entire universe of meaning where language and society interpenetrate the lived value of words.

Language, like culture, is often regarded as a tool or an instrument of thought. But then language is a tool which accomplishes far more and yet is far less logical than we may like it to be. It is full of ambiguity and in general far too luxuriant for the taste of positivist philosophers. As a tool, language seems to use us as much as we use it. In this, it is more like the rest of our culture, which we cannot use without inhabiting it. Ultimately, language and culture defeat any attempt to conceive them as a system capable of revealing the genesis of its own meaning. This is because we *are* the language we are talking about. That is, we are the ground of language through our body. It is through our body that we can speak of the world, because the world in turn speaks to us through the body.

> "In my book the body lives in and moves through space and is the home of a full human personality. The words I write are adapted to express first one of its functions then another. In *Lestrygonians* the stomach dominates and the rhythm of the episode is that of the peristaltic movement." "But the minds, the thoughts of the characters," I began. "If they had no body they would have no mind," said Joyce. "It's all one. Walking towards his lunch my hero, Leopold Bloom, thinks of his wife, and says to himself, 'Molly's legs are out of plumb.' At another time of day he might have expressed the same thought without any underthought of food. But I want the reader to understand always through suggestion rather than direct statement." [10]

We may distinguish between the institution of *language*, as an objective structure studied by linguistics, and *speech*, which is the use-value language acquires when turned toward expression

10. Frank Budgen, *James Joyce and the Making of Ulysses* (Bloomington: Indiana University Press, 1960), p. 21.

and the institution of new meanings.[11] We start by reading an author, a philosopher or a novelist, leaning at first upon the common associations of his words, until, gradually, the words begin to flow in us and to open us to an original sound which is the writer's voice borrowing from us an understanding that until then we did not know was ours to offer. Yet it comes only from what we ourselves brought to the book, our knowledge of the language and of ourselves, and life's questions that we share with the author. Once we have acquired the author's style of thinking, our lives interweave in a presence which is the anticipation of the whole of the author's intention and its simultaneous recovery which continues the understanding. In talking with and listening to one another, we make an accommodation through language and the body in which we grow older together. We encroach upon one another borrowing from each other's time, words, and looks what we are looking for in ourselves. In this way our mind and self may be thought of as an *institution* which we inhabit with others in a system of presences which includes Socrates or Sartre just as much as our friends in the room.

> When I speak or understand, I experience that presence of others in myself or of myself in others which is the stumbling-block of the theory of intersubjectivity. I experience that presence of what is represented which is the stumbling-block of the theory of time, and I finally understand what is meant by Husserl's enigmatic statement, "Transcendental subjectivity is intersubjectivity." To the extent that what I say has meaning, I am a different "other" for myself when I am speaking; and to the extent that I understand, I no longer know who is speaking and who is listening.[12]

Expression is always an act of self-improvisation in which we borrow from the world, from others, and from our own past efforts. Language is the child in us who speaks of the world in order to know who he is. Through language I discover myself

11. Maurice Merleau-Ponty, "On the Phenomenology of Language," in *Signs*, trans. Richard C. McCleary (Evanston: Northwestern University Press, 1964), pp. 86–87. See Edie's comments on the distinction between *la langue* et *la parole* in "Was Merleau-Ponty a Structuralist?," p. 305.

12. *Signs*, p. 97.

and others, in talking, listening, reading, and writing. It is language which makes possible that aesthetic distance between myself and the world through which I can speak about the world and the world in turn speak in me. Our thoughts and purposes are embodied in bodily gestures which in the act of expression structure themselves toward habit and spontaneity, and thus we make our world.

Merleau-Ponty's relation to Saussure's structural linguistics is typical of the way he treated all his "sources." He was concerned with the semantic and even more, as his own thought progressed, with the ontological implications of language. We must remember this if we are to avoid fruitless arguments over the documentation, in the conventional sense, of texts used by Merleau-Ponty. We otherwise miss the philosopher at work, improvising that new style of philosophical work for which Husserl called in *The Crisis*.[13] The concern with philosophical sources henceforth, that is, in view of the surrender of philosophy to *technique*, must be a concern with the very possibility of philosophy and its world.

I believe that we must try to understand Merleau-Ponty's patient analyses of the idealist and realist or subjectivist and naturalist accounts of perception, language, and history as efforts to understand the history of philosophy itself as the history of world domination whose substructures are science and capital accumulation. Perhaps this approach will enable us to understand the *ambiguity* of Merleau-Ponty's thought. This does not mean what it might ordinarily suggest for the reader's experience with Merleau-Ponty's writings. After all, at least since Sartre the question of how we read a text has no simple answer. The ambiguity of Merleau-Ponty's thought is properly the ambiguity in the tradition of Western philosophy which has elaborated solipsistic and intersubjectivist, nominalist and essentialist, subjectivist and objectivist accounts of the *same* phenomenal world.

If we regard the experience of ambiguity at all seriously, it means that the truth of philosophy is the work of generations of philosophers linked as much by what they reject as by what

13. Husserl, *Crisis*, p. 351.

they affirm. In other words, we shall understand the *institution of philosophy*.[14] But this is a conception which appears dangerously close to the end of philosophy. The names of Kierkegaard, Marx, and Nietzsche remind us of the denial of philosophy since Hegel and that with them "we enter an age of nonphilosophy."[15] Nowadays, philosophical reflection no longer spreads its wings but must tread the earth wearily, amazed at its own variety, its own potential for barbarism. Reason must confront its own violence in the new extremes of naturalism and artificialism which seem capable of producing once and for all man's world alienation in a way that far exceeds the anticipations of nineteenth-century historicism and relativism.

But the concern with the "crisis" of Western rationalism as it is approached by Husserl does not produce an existentialist despair or an irrational reversal. These are symptomatic phenomena which threaten to divert the philosopher from the really necessary undertaking of a "teleological-historical reflection upon the origins of our critical scientific and philosophical situation." The philosopher, says Husserl, "takes something from history." But history is not a warehouse or a rummage heap from which we can take "things," because facts, documents, philosophical and literary works, are not palpably before us, apart from our own indwelling and interpretations. Furthermore, we do not, strictly speaking, transmit or hand down a scientific, literary, or historical tradition. We may be Renaissance historians without having read or researched every aspect of the Renaissance, just as we may be Platonists without a concern for every word of Plato, so that we may as well speak of a "poetic transmission" which owes as much to us as to fact. And yet none of this need imperil the teleology of knowledge, of science, history, or philosophy.

> Let us be more precise. I know, of course, what I am striving for under the title of philosophy, as the goal and field of my work.

14. O'Neill, *Perception, Expression*, chap. 5.

15. Maurice Merleau-Ponty, "Philosophy as Interrogation," *Themes from the Lectures at the Collège de France 1952–1960*, trans. John O'Neill (Evanston: Northwestern University Press, 1970), p. 100.

> And yet I do not know. What autonomous thinker has ever been satisfied with this, his "knowledge"? For what autonomous thinker, in his philosophizing life, has "philosophy" ever ceased to be an enigma? Everyone has the sense of philosophy's end, to whose realization his life is devoted; everyone has certain formulae, expressed in definitions; but only secondary thinkers, who in truth should not be called philosophers, are consoled by their definitions, beating to death with their word-concepts the problematic *telos* of philosophizing. In that obscure "knowledge," and in the word-concepts of the formulae, the historical is concealed; it is, according to its own proper sense, the spiritual inheritance of him who philosophizes; and in the same way, obviously, he understands the others in whose company, in critical friendship and enmity, he philosophizes. And in philosophizing he is also in company with himself as he earlier understood and did philosophy; and he knows that, in the process, historical tradition, as he understood it and used it, entered into him in a motivating way and as a spiritual sediment. His historical picture, in part made by himself and in part taken over, his "poetic invention of the history of philosophy," has not and does not remain fixed—that he knows; and yet every "invention" serves him and can serve him in understanding himself and his aim, and his own aim in relation to that of others and their "inventions," their aims, and finally what it is that is common to all, which makes up philosophy "as such" as a unitary *telos* and makes the systems attempts at its fulfillment for us all, for us [who are] at the same time in company with the philosophers of the past (in the various ways we have been able to invent them for ourselves).[16]

Understood in this way, rational argument, discovery, and criticism lie within the tradition and community of philosophers, artists, and natural and social scientists. This is a conception of the contingency of philosophical reason which avoids the postures of the alienated critic and the nihilistic dangers of cultural relativism while nevertheless providing for each thinker's style and for the local thrust of culture.

Merleau-Ponty remarks how well Husserl's term *Stiftung*, foundation or institution, captures the fecundity of cultural creations by which they endure into our present and open a field of inquiry to which they are continuously relevant.

16. Husserl, *Crisis*, pp. 394–95.

> It is thus that the world as soon as he has seen it, his first attempts at painting, and the whole past of painting all deliver up a *tradition* to the painter—*that is,* Husserl remarks, *the power to forget origins* and to give to the past not a survival, which is the hypocritical form of forgetfulness, but a new life, which is the noble form of memory.[17]

Through language, art, and writing, what was only an ideal meaning in the mind of an individual achieves an objective and public status, enters a community of thinkers, which is the presupposition of truth. Thus we witness the event of that circuit of reflection in which what was first recognized as neither local nor temporal "according to the meaning of its being" comes to rest upon the locality and temporality of speech, which belongs neither to the objective world nor the world of ideas.

> Ideal existence is based upon the document. Not, undoubtedly, upon the document as a physical object, or even as the vehicle of one-to-one significations assigned to it by the language it is written in. But ideal existence is based upon the document insofar as (still through an "intentional transgression") the document solicits and brings together all knowing lives—and as such establishes and re-establishes a "Logos" of the cultural world.[18]

From the crisis of reason Husserl produces a conception of the limits of philosophical reflexivity that is consistent with the movement of "poetic invention" (*Dichtung*) as well as with the community in which we philosophize. This in turn underlies Merleau-Ponty's concept of reflexivity as *institution* rather than as transcendental constitution. The notion of institution is the ground of a conception of reflexivity which, instead of resting upon a transcendental subjectivity, is given in a field of presence and coexistence which situates reflexivity and truth as sedimentation and search. We must think of reflexivity as tied to the textual structures of temporality and situation through which subjectivity and objectivity are constituted as the intentional unity and style of the world.[19]

> Thus what we understand by the concept of institution are those events in experience which endow it with durable dimen-

17. *Signs*, p. 59.
18. *Ibid.*, pp. 96–97.
19. John O'Neill, "Situation and Temporality," *Philosophy and Phenomenological Research*, XXVIII, no. 3 (March, 1968), 413–22.

> sions, in relation to which a whole series of other experiences will acquire meaning, will form an intelligible series or a history—or again those events which sediment in me a meaning, not just as survivals or residues, but as the invitation to a sequel, the necessity of a future.[20]

The institution of reflexivity operates through a series of exchanges between subjectivity and situation in which the polarities of means and ends or question and answer are continuously established and renewed, thereby sedimenting ideas, truth, and culture. Reflexivity, therefore, is not an a priori but a task which we take up in order to achieve self-improvisation as well as the acquisition of a tradition or style of thought which is the recovery of an original auspices opened in the past. To this we bring a living expression, or the inauguration of a world and the outline of a future which is nothing else than ourselves, "borne only by the caryatid of our efforts, which converge by the sole fact that they are efforts to express." [21]

The institution of philosophy is the result of abandoning Husserl's attempt to construct a presuppositionless science as the correlative of an unsituated and unhistorical subjectivity, with all its problems for intersubjectivity, rationality, and philosophy itself—the realization that the corpus of knowledge, literature, art, and music is produced by individuals who take up a tradition of inquiry which is never settled and yet never wholly in doubt. Thus the philosopher, the artist, and the critic are always in debt, while giving more than they have ever received. For this reason, they proceed in their work as much by going back to the original questions in their field as by turning their backs on it, dreaming only of unheard and unseen things. This is not a simplistic argument for eternal starts any more than it is a crude rejection of the accumulation of knowledge. It is rather an attempt to interpret the solicitation and response through which tradition and rebellion are made.[22]

20. Maurice Merleau-Ponty, "Institution in Personal and Public History," in *Themes from the Lectures*, pp. 40–41.

21. *Signs*, p. 69.

22. The argument upon which I have drawn here is developed more fully in my essay "Can Phenomenology Be Critical?," *Philosophy of the Social Sciences*, II, no. 1 (March, 1972), 1–13.

What phenomenology recovers for us and thus what it introduces us to is not just the freshness of perception or the novelty of language and art, though it surely reveals these as openings among the world, ourselves, and others. In Merleau-Ponty's hands, phenomenology is also the recovery of the tradition of reason in philosophy, politics, and history. In this he continues the task of *responsible rationality*[23] invoked by Husserl in *The Crisis of European Sciences.* Whether we follow Husserl in taking stock of the predicament of modern philosophy or analyzing the prejudice of the natural attitude or whether we follow Merleau-Ponty in attempting to refashion the Marxist philosophy of history on the basis of his critique of scientism,[24] we are engaged in the program of revealing the historical discourse of rationality and the philosopher's own itinerary as collective efforts to which we must be responsible without ever reducing this commitment to a methodical certitude.

For this reason, we do not find in *The Prose of the World,* any more than in other words of Merleau-Ponty, an exposition of method. By the same token, what we find of this in working notes and programatic statements does not lie there through any failure of inclusion or organization but stands as it is—the trace of a philosopher's working life to be understood the way he himself spoke of the artist's sketches. These are not elements of some master painting the artist had in mind—that is precisely the

23. "We have also become aware in the most general way that human philosophizing and its results in the whole of man's existence mean anything but merely private or otherwise limited cultural goals. In *our* philosophizing, then—how can we avoid it?—we are *functionaries of mankind.* The quite personal responsibility of our own true being as philosophers, our inner personal vocation, bears within itself at the same time the responsibility for the true being of mankind; the latter is, necessarily, being toward a *telos* and can only come to realization, *if at all,* through philosophy—through *us, if* we are philosophers in all seriousness. Is there, in this existential 'if,' a way out? If not, what should we, who *believe,* do in order to *be able* to believe? We cannot seriously continue our previous philosophizing; it lets us hope only for philosophies, never for philosophy" (Husserl, *Crisis,* p. 17).

24. Maurice Merleau-Ponty, *Humanism and Terror: An Essay on the Communist Problem,* trans. John O'Neill (Boston: Beacon Press, 1969).

fiction of the reviewer, whether art reviewer or philosophical reviewer. The latter presupposes some ground from which the author's intention can be viewed either in back of him or ahead of him but never given to him as it is to the critic. But this is to dispose of the author in favor of Philosophy or Art, to abort the artist's life and the philosopher's labor as failures of total perception, trapped in perspective and situation. In this we are bewitched, by language and its power of reification, to make prose of the world at the expense of its poetry.

The philosopher, like the painter or writer, must know how to assimilate the accumulation of tradition, style, and form in order to make an expressive use of them the way he moves his body without a precise concern for its anatomical and neurological structure without which every gesture is impossible. The true philosopher has philosophy in his bones, but these are not a dead man's bones. Philosophy is his life, the flesh of his thought through which he is open to the thoughts of other thinkers, exposed to their moods and times while still belonging to his own. The tradition in which he lives advances by a "poetic transmission" between the universal and the particular, between him and everyman.

> The Museum kills the vehemence of painting just as the library, as Sartre says, transforms writings which were once a man's gestures into *messages*. It is the historicity of death. But there is a living historicity of which the Museum offers only a broken image. It is the historicity that dwells in the painter at work when, in a single gesture, he binds the tradition he continues into the tradition he founds. It is the historicity which in a single stroke joins him with everything that has ever been painted in the world, without his having to leave either his place or time, or his blessed and accursed labor. The true history of painting is not one which puts painting in the past and then invokes superartists and fatalities—it is the history that puts everything in the present, that dwells in artists and reintegrates the painter with the fraternity of painters.[25]

It is in terms of the struggle between the two historicities of life and death that we must approach Merleau-Ponty's reflections on the algorithmic structure of language and the production of

25. *The Prose of the World*, p. 73.

meaning in talk and literature. Although Merleau-Ponty recognized the existence of grammatical structures which subsist in our speech, he considered the Husserlian notion of an "eidetics" of language a forlorn attempt to escape the intrinsic historicity of all languages. Yet Merleau-Ponty is far from rejecting the idea of a universal discourse between men. Indeed, the very reason that he rejects a scientistic linguistic base for a universal discourse is that it subverts the subjective, historical, and political responsibility which is the ground of such discourse.

Thus, as James Edie remarks, the question in Merleau-Ponty is not whether there are some linguistic universals, but what *kind* of universality we can find in language.[26] Merleau-Ponty was quite aware of the empirical facts of the translatability of languages and of their individual completeness in expressing their own worlds. But he understood the relation between the surface and deep structure of language (though these are not his expressions) in terms of a teleology of reason which is realized only through the experience of history and language in the production of a logic within contingency—an incarnate logic.

> Advent does not leave time behind: it is a promise of events. The domination of the many by the one in the history of painting, such as we have met in the exercise of the perceiving body, does not consummate succession in an eternity. On the contrary, domination demands succession; domination needs succession at the same time that it grounds its signification. Between the two problems there is more than a simple *analogy*. It is the expressive operation of the body, begun in the least perception, which amplifies into painting and art. The field of pictorial significations was opened the moment a man appeared in the world. The first sketch on the walls of a cave founded a tradition only because it gleaned from another—the tradition of perception. The quasi eternity of art compounds the quasi eternity of our corporeal existence. It is through our body that we have the first experience of the impalpable body of history prior to all initiation into art.[27]

26. "Was Merleau-Ponty a Structuralist?," pp. 317–18. Edie's argument should be consulted in detail as well as for some marvelous passages from Merleau-Ponty on language and "singing" the world.

27. *The Prose of the World*, pp. 82–83.

The transcendence of language, thought, and art is not husbanded by making it a factual transcendent. It is a *work* of ours, a task we continuously initiate and collectively elaborate producing new sense, new perceptions upon wave after wave of meaning, which ebbs and flows nowhere else than from ourselves.

> True history thus gets its life entirely from us. It is in our present that true history gets the force to refer everything else to the present. The *other* whom I respect gets his life from me as I get my life from him. A philosophy of history does not deprive me of any rights and privileges. It simply adds to my personal obligations the obligation to understand situations other than my own and to create a path between my life and the lives of others, that is, to express myself. The lines between one life and another are not traced in advance. It is through the action of culture that I come to abide in lives that are not mine. I confront them, I reveal them to one another, I make them share equally in an order of truth. Responsible for all of them, I awaken a universal life—just as in one fell swoop I assume my place in space through the live and dense presence of my body.[28]

The universality and truth toward which theoretical consciousness aims are not an intrinsic property of the Idea. They are an acquisition continuously established and reestablished in a community and tradition of knowledge for which individuals in specific historical situations call and to which they respond. Understood in this way, history is the call of one thought to another, because each individual's work or action is created across the path of self and others toward a *public* which it elicits rather than serves. That is, history is the field which individual effort requires in order to become one with the community it seeks to build, so that where it is successful its invention appears always to have been necessary. Individual action, then, is the invention of history, because it is shaped in a present which previously was not just a void waiting to be determined by the word or deed but a tissue of calling and response which is the life of no one and everyone. Every one of life's actions, insofar as it invokes its truth, lives in the expectation of an historical inscription, a judg-

28. *Ibid.*, pp. 86–87.

ment not only of its intention or consequences but also of its fecundity—the relevance of its "story" to the present.

> History is the judge—not History as the Power of a moment or of a century, but history as the space of inscription and accumulation beyond the limits of countries and epochs of what we have said and done that is most true and valuable, taking into account the circumstances in which we had to speak. Others will judge what I have done, because I painted the painting to be seen, because my action committed the future of others; but neither art nor politics consists in pleasing or flattering others. What they expect of the artist or politician is that he draw them toward values in which they will only later recognize their own values. The painter or politician shapes others more often than he follows them. The *public* at whom he aims is not given; it is a public to be elicited by his work. The others of whom he thinks are not empirical "others" or even *humanity* conceived as a species; it is others once they have become such that he can live with them. The history in which the artist participates (and it is better the less he thinks about "making history" and honestly produces *his* work as he sees it) is not a power before which he must genuflect. It is the perpetual conversation woven together by all speech, all valid works and actions, each, according to its place and circumstance, contesting and confirming the other, each one re-creating all the others.[29]

Merleau-Ponty returns philosophy to the flux of the natural and historical world, rejecting its compromise with the ideals of objectivism which have made the tradition of rationality an enigma to itself. Henceforth, philosophy must abide in the life-world where Husserl had found its roots and from there it must recover its own ontological history. The *Crisis* is, of course, the prime example of this effort to reflect upon the history of Western rationality *without breaking with the natural attitude* and yet not resulting in a conventional empirical history of philosophy. It is the model, I believe, for Merleau-Ponty's own efforts in uncovering the ontological history of perception and expression in art, literature, language, and philosophy.

Paul Ricoeur has seriously questioned whether Husserlian phenomenology can be turned toward the task of its own his-

29. *Ibid.*, p. 86.

torical understanding.[30] David Carr, introducing his translation of the *Crisis* also draws attention to the Hegelian mode of this question but remarks that the "crisis" theme is unthinkable in terms of the Hegelian "theodicy." But it is just here that we need to keep in mind Husserl's insistence that we must rethink the past of philosophy, and in this case with whom should we be more concerned than Hegel? It is surely not an easy task to read Hegel. For the same reason, it is not obvious whether Husserl is at fault in raising the Hegelian question. Merleau-Ponty appears not to have thought so. However, he saw in *The Phenomenology of Spirit* not simply a history of ideas forced into a procrustean bed of categories but the history of reason in the life-worlds of moral, economic, political, and philosophical experience. Throughout this history the forms of sense-certitude, understanding, and reason are embedded in the most basic structure of the life-world, namely, the dialectic of recognition and the struggle to death which shapes the tragic course of human rationality as a social, historical, and political enterprise that is not simply a goal of philosophy.

> So the Hegelian dialectic is what we call the phenomenon of expression, which gathers itself step by step and launches itself again through the mystery of rationality. We would undoubtedly recover the true sense of the concept of history if we acquired the habit of modeling it on the example of the arts and language. The close connection between each expression and every other within a single order instituted by the first act of expression effects the junction of the individual and the universal. Expression—language, for example—is what most belongs to us as individuals, for while addressing itself to others, it simultaneously acquires a universal value. The central fact to which the Hegelian dialectic returns in a hundred ways is that we do not have to choose between the *pour soi* and the *pour autrui*, between our own version of thought and the version of others, which is alienation itself, because at the moment of expression the other to whom I address myself and I who express myself are linked without concession on either side. The others, such as they are or will be, are not the sole judges of what I do. If I wanted to deny myself for their benefit, I

30. Paul Ricoeur, "Husserl and the Sense of History," in his *Husserl: An Analysis of His Phenomenology* (Evanston: Northwestern University Press, 1967).

would deny them too as "self." They are worth exactly what I am worth, and all the powers I accord to them I give simultaneously to myself. I submit myself to the judgment of another who is *himself worthy of what I have attempted,* that is, in the last analysis, to the judgment of a peer whom I myself have chosen.[31]

The recovery of the ontological history of rationality is therefore not simply gained through the critique of objectivism and naturalism exercised through the phenomenological reduction. It involves a return to the prephilosophical logos of the world which is the mystery and the wonder upon which our communally naïve and theoretical lives build equally.[32] But this need not be a further exercise in the ahistorical mystification of reason.[33] It is precisely the violent assumption of the responsibility of reason which lies nowhere else than with ourselves.

JOHN O'NEILL

31. *The Prose of the World,* pp. 85–86.

32. John O'Neill, "Hegel and Marx on History as Human History," in Jean Hyppolite, *Studies on Marx and Hegel,* trans. John O'Neill (London: Heinemann Educational Books, 1969).

33. Aron Gurwitsch, "The Last Work of Edmund Husserl," in his *Studies in Phenomenology and Psychology* (Evanston: Northwestern University Press, 1966), pp. 445–47.

The Prose of the World

1 / The Specter of a Pure Language

MEN HAVE BEEN TALKING for a long time on earth, and yet three-quarters of what they say goes unnoticed. *A rose, it is raining, it is fine, man is mortal.* These are paradigms of expression for us. We believe expression is most complete when it points unequivocally to events, to states of objects, to ideas or relations, for, in these instances, expression leaves nothing more to be desired, contains nothing which it does not reveal, and thus sweeps us toward the object which it designates. In dialogue, narrative, plays on words, trust, promise, prayer, eloquence, literature, we possess a second-order language in which we do not speak of objects and ideas except to reach some person. Words respond to words in this language, which bears away within itself and builds up beyond nature a humming, busy world of its own. Yet we still insist on treating this language as simply a variant of the economical forms of making statements about some *thing.* Thus expression involves nothing more than replacing a perception or an idea with a conventional sign that announces, evokes, or abridges it. Of course, language contains more than just ready-made phrases and can refer to what has never yet been seen. But how could language achieve this if what is new were not composed of old elements already experienced—that is, if new relations were not entirely definable through the vocabulary and syntactical relations of the conventional language? A language makes use of a certain number of basic signs, arbitrarily linked to certain key significations. From the latter it can recompose any new significations and can thus express them in the same language. Finally, a language expresses something because it channels all our experiences into the system of initial correspondences between a particular sign and the particular signification which we acquired when learning the language. The language itself is absolutely clear because not a single thought is left trailing behind the words or any word behind the pure thought of some object. We all secretly venerate the ideal of a language which in the last analysis would deliver us from language by delivering us to things. We regard language as a fabulous apparatus which enables us to express an indefinite number of thoughts or objects through a finite number of signs chosen so as to recompose exactly everything new that one may wish to say and to bestow upon it the same evidence as the primary designations of things.

Since the apparatus works, since one does in fact speak and write, it is thought that language (like God's understanding) contains the germs of every conceivable signification and that all our thoughts are destined to be expressed in language; or that every signification which enters man's experience carries within it its own formula, as the sun, in the minds of Piaget's children, bears its name in its center. Our language recovers, in the heart of things, the word which made the thing.

These are not just common-sense attitudes. They predominate in the exact sciences (but not, as we shall see, in linguistics). It is frequently repeated that science is a well-formed language. This means also that language is the beginning of science and that the algorithm is the mature form of language. Now, science attaches clear and precise significations to fixed signs. It fixes a certain number of transparent relations and, to represent them, it establishes symbols which in themselves are meaningless and can therefore never say more than they mean conventionally. Having thus protected itself from the shifts in meaning which create error, science is in principle assured at any moment of being able completely to justify its claims by appealing to its initial definitions. Whenever there is a question of expressing, in the same algorithm, relations for which it was not constructed—the so-called problems of another form—it may be necessary to introduce new definitions and new symbols. But if the algorithm is to do its job, if it means to be a rigorous language and to control its moves at every moment, nothing implicit should be introduced into it. All new and all old relations should form one family, derivable from a single system of possible relations, so that one never means to say more than one does say and no more is said than one means. Then, finally, the sign remains a simple abbreviation of a thought which could at any moment clarify and explain itself. Thus the sole but decisive virtue of expression is to replace the confused allusions which each of our thoughts makes to all the others with precise significations for which we may truly be responsible, because their exact sense is known to us. The virtue of expression is to recover for us the life of our thought. Likewise, the expressive value of the algorithm is lodged entirely in the unequivocal relations between secondary and primitive significations and between primitive significations and signs that in themselves have no signification—where our thought discovers nothing but what it has put into them.

The algorithm, the project of a universal language, is a revolt against language in its existing state and a refusal to depend upon the confusions of everyday language. The algorithm is an attempt to construct language according to the standard of truth, to redefine it to match the divine mind, and to return to the very origin of the history of speech or, rather, to tear speech out of history. The divine speech, or the language we always presuppose as prior to speech, is no longer to be found in modern languages scattered throughout history and the world. The internal word is the standard of the external word. In this sense, the internal word is the very opposite of the magical belief which puts the word "sun" in the center of the sun. All the same, language was created by God at the beginning of the world; it was sent forth by him and received by us as a prophecy. Prefigured in God's understanding by the system of possibles which preeminently contains our confused world, language is rediscovered in human thought. In the name of this spiritual model, human thought puts order into the chaos of historical languages. Thus in every instance language resembles the objects and ideas expressed in it. Language is the double of being, and we cannot conceive of an object or idea that comes into the world without words. Mythical or intelligible, there is a place where everything that now exists or will exist prepares itself for being put into words.

In the writer, this is a fixed belief. One should always go back to those astonishing words which Jean Paulhan cites from La Bruyère: "Of all the possible expressions which might render our thought, there is only one which is the best. One does not always come upon it in writing or talking: it is nevertheless true that it exists."[1] How does he know this? He knows that the writer or speaker is first mute, straining toward what he wants to convey, toward what he is *going to say.* Then suddenly a flood of words comes to save this muteness and gives it an equivalent so exact and so capable of yielding the writer's own thought to him when he may have forgotten it, that one can only believe that the thought had been expressed before the world began. Language is there, like an all-purpose tool, with its vocabulary, its turns of phrase and form which have been so useful, and it always responds to our call, ready to express anything, because language is the treasury of everything one may wish to say—because language has all our future experience already written into it, just as the destiny of men is written in the stars. All that is required is to meet the phrase ready made in the limbs of language, to recover the muted language in which being murmurs to us. It may seem that our friends, being who they are, could not be called by any other names, that in naming them we simply deciphered what was required by eyes that color, a face like that, that walk—though some are misnamed and all their lives carry a false name or pseudonym (like a wig or mask). In the same way, an expression and what it expresses strangely alternate and, through a sort of false recognition, make us feel that the word has inhabited the thing from all eternity.

But if men unearth a prehistoric language spoken in things, or if beneath our stammerings there is a golden age of language in which words once adhered to the objects themselves, then communication involves no mystery. I point to a world around

1. Jean Paulhan, *Les Fleurs de Tarbes* (Paris: Gallimard, 1941), p. 128.

me which already speaks, just as I point my finger toward an object already in the visual field of others. It is said that physiognomic expressions are equivocal in themselves and that blushing may indicate pleasure, shame, anger, or passion, according to the context. In the same way, a linguistic gesticulation may arouse nothing in the mind of an observer, because it shows him in silence things whose name he already knows because he is their name. But let us leave aside the myth of a language of things, or, rather, let us take it in its sublime form, as a universal language which contains in advance everything it may have to express, because its words and syntax reflect the fundamental possibles and their articulations. The implications are the same. The word possesses no virtue of its own; there is no power hidden in it. It is a pure sign standing for a pure signification. The person speaking is coding his thought. He replaces his thought with a visible or sonorous pattern which is nothing but sounds in the air or ink spots on the paper. Thought understands itself and is self-sufficient. Thought signifies outside itself through a message which does not carry it and conveys it unequivocally only to another mind, which can read the message because it attaches the same signification to the same sign, whether by habit, by human conventions, or by divine institution. In any case, we never find among other people's words any that we have not put there ourselves. Communication is an appearance; it never brings us anything truly new. How could communication possibly carry us beyond our own powers of reflection, since the signs communication employs could never tell us anything unless we already grasped the signification? It may be true that when we watch signals in the night, like Fabrice, or the fast- and slow-moving letters in a flashing neon sign, we feel we are watching the birth of the news. Something pulsates and comes alive: the thought of a man shrouded somewhere in the distance. But, actually, this is only a mirage. If I were not present to perceive the rhythm and pick out the moving letters, there would be only a meaningless mechanical clicking on and off of lights, like the twinkling of the stars. Even the news of a death or a disaster brought to me by telegram is not entirely news; I receive this news only because I already know that *deaths* and *disasters* are possible. Certainly, there is something more than just this in the way men *experience* language. They cannot restrain themselves from chatting with a famous author. They visit him the way people visit St. Peter's statue. They have a mute faith in the secret virtues of communication. They do not need to be told that news is news. They know that it helps nothing to have thought often of death, so long as one has not learned of the death of a loved one. But the moment people begin to reflect upon language instead of living it, they cannot see how language can have such power. After all, we understand what is said to us because we know in advance the meaning of the words spoken to us.* We understand only what we already know and never set ourselves any problem that we are not able to resolve. Consider the model of two thinking subjects closed in their significations—between them messages circulate which convey nothing and are only the occasion for each subject to observe what he already knew—and when the one speaks and the other listens, their thoughts reproduce one another, but unwittingly and never face to face. Such a theory of language would result ultimately (as Paulhan says), "in everything happening between them *as though language had not existed.*" [2]

* Describe the contrast between meaning which is at hand and meaning which is in the process of creation.

2. Paulhan, *Fleurs de Tarbes,* p. 128.

2 / Science and the Experience of Expression

Now, ONE OF THE EFFECTS of language is to efface itself to the extent that its expression comes across. As I become engrossed in a book, I no longer see the letters on the page or recall turning each page. Through all the letters, and on every page, I continually seek and find the "same" incidents, the "same" events, even to the point of not noticing the light or perspective in which they are presented. Similarly, in naïve perception, I see a man over there who has a man's shape, although I can describe his "apparent size" only by closing one eye, fragmenting the visual field, destroying the background, and projecting the whole spectacle onto a single illusory plane where every fragment is compared to some close object, such as my pencil, and thus assigned a specific size. It is impossible to make the comparison with both eyes open. Then my pencil is a near object and things far away are far away, and between them and my pencil there is no common reference. Or, rather, if I succeed in making the comparison for one object in the visual field, I cannot simultaneously manage it for the other objects. The man over there is neither one inch nor five feet tall; he is a man in the distance. There his height is like a meaning which lies within him but not like an observable trait, for I am totally unaware of any signs by which I may spot it. In the same way, a great book, a play, or a poem is in my memory *en bloc*. I can, of course, by recalling what I have read or heard, remember a particular passage, word, situation, or shift in the action. But when I do this, I am dealing with a recollection which is unique and retains its evidence independently of these details, for it is as unique and as inexhaustible as the sight of an object. When a conversation involves me and for a time gives me the feeling of really talking to someone, I forget none of it. The next day I can relate it to anyone interested in it. But if it really excites me as a book can, I do not have to recollect a series of quite distinct events. I still have it in my hands like something I hold, wrapped up, in my memory. For everything—the interlocutor's gestures, his smiles, his hesitations, and his words—to reappear in its proper place, all I must do is remember the incident. When someone—an author or a friend—succeeds in expressing himself, the signs are immediately forgotten; all that remains is the meaning. The perfection of language lies in its capacity to pass unnoticed.

But therein lies the virtue of language: it is language which propels us toward the things it signifies. In the way it works, language hides itself from us. Its triumph is to efface itself and to take us beyond the words to the author's very thoughts, so that we imagine we are engaged with him in a wordless meeting of minds. Once the words have cooled and been reaffixed to the page as signs, their very power to project us far away from themselves makes it impossible for us to believe they are the source of so many thoughts. Nevertheless, while we were reading, it is these words which spoke to us, suspended in the movement of our eyes and our feelings, which they in turn carried and projected unerringly when they rejoined in us the blind man and the paralytic, when they, thanks to us, and we, thanks to them, became speech rather than language, and in the same instant became a voice and its echo.

We may say that there are two languages. First, there is language after the fact, or language as an institution, which effaces itself in order to yield the meaning which it conveys. Second, there is the language which creates itself in its expressive acts, which sweeps me on from the signs toward meaning—sedimented language and speech.[1]

1. TRANSLATOR: . . . *le langage parlé et le langage parlant.*

Once I have read *the* book, it acquires a unique and palpable existence quite apart from the words on the pages. It is with reference to the book that I discover the details I am seeking. One may even say that, while I am reading the book, it is always with reference to the whole, as I grasp it at any point, that I understand each phrase, each shift in the narrative or delay in the action, to the point where, as the reader, I feel, in Sartre's words, as though I have written the book from start to finish.[2] But that is an afterthought. In reality, I could not have written the book which I love so much. In reality, one must read it first and then, as Sartre again puts it so well, it "catches" like a fire.[3] I bring the match near, I light a flimsy piece of paper, and, behold, my gesture receives inspired help from the things around, as if the chimney and the dry wood had been waiting for me to set the light, or as though the match had been nothing but a magic incantation, a call of like to like answered beyond all imagination. In the same way, I start to read a book idly, giving it hardly any thought; and suddenly, a few words move me, the fire catches, my thoughts are ablaze, there is nothing in the book which I can overlook, and the fire feeds off everything I have ever read. I am receiving and giving in the same gesture. I have given my knowledge of the language; I have brought along what I already know about the meaning of the words, the phrases, and the syntax. I have also contributed my whole experience of others and everyday events, with all the questions it left in me—the situations left open and unsettled, as well as those with whose ordinary resolution I am all too familiar.

But the book would not interest me so much if it only told me about things I already know. It makes use of everything I have contributed in order to carry me beyond it. With the aid of signs agreed upon by the author and myself because we speak the same language, the book makes me believe that we had already shared a common stock of well-worn and readily available significations. The author has come to dwell in my world. Then,

2. Jean-Paul Sartre, *What Is Literature?*, trans. Bernard Frechtman (New York: Harper & Row, 1965), chap. 2.

3. *Ibid.*, p. 37.

imperceptibly, he varies the ordinary meaning of the signs, and like a whirlwind they sweep me along toward the other meaning with which I am going to connect.

Before I read Stendhal, I know what a rogue is. Thus I can understand what he means when he says that Rossi the revenue man is a rogue. But when Rossi the rogue begins to live, it is no longer he who is a rogue: it is a rogue who is the revenue man Rossi. I have access to Stendhal's outlook through the commonplace words he uses. But in his hands, these words are given a new twist. The cross references multiply. More and more arrows point in the direction of a thought I have never encountered before and perhaps never would have met without Stendhal. At the same time, the contexts in which Stendhal uses common words reveal even more majestically the new meaning with which he endows them. I get closer and closer to him, until in the end I read his words with the very same intention that he gave to them. One cannot mimic a person's voice without assuming something of his physiognomy and even his personal style. In the same way, the author's voice results in my assuming his thoughts. Common words and familiar events, like jealousy or a duel, which at first immerse us in everyone's world, suddenly function as emissaries from Stendhal's world. Although the final effect is not for me to dwell within Stendhal's lived experience, I am at least brought within the imaginary self and the internal dialogue Stendhal held with it for the fifty years he was coining it in his works. It is only then that the reader or the author can say with Paulhan, "In this light at least, I have been you." [4]

I create Stendhal; I am Stendhal while reading him. But that is because first he knew how to bring me to dwell within him. The reader's sovereignty is only imaginary, since he draws all his force from that infernal machine called the book, the apparatus for making significations. The relations between the reader and the book are like those loves in which one partner initially dominates because he was more proud or more temperamental, and then the situation changes and the other, more wise and more silent,

4. Jean Paulhan, *Les Fleurs de Tarbes* (Paris: Gallimard, 1941), p. 133.

rules. The expressive moment occurs where the relationship reverses itself, where the book takes possession of the reader.

Sedimented language is the language the reader brings with him, the stock of accepted relations between signs and familiar significations without which he could never have begun to read. It constitutes the language and the literature of the language. Thus it is also Stendhal's work once it has been understood and added to the cultural heritage.

But speech is the book's call to the unprejudiced reader. Speech is the operation through which a certain arrangement of already available signs and significations alters and then transfigures each of them, so that in the end a new signification is secreted. It is the effect through which Stendhal's own language comes to life in the reader's mind, henceforth for the reader's own use. Once I have acquired this language, I can easily delude myself into believing that I could have understood it by myself, because it has transformed me and made me capable of understanding it.

In afterthought, everything happens as though in effect language had not existed. Moreover, I flatter myself with being able to understand Stendhal from my own thoughts, and at most I grudgingly concede him a part of the system—like those who repay old debts by borrowing from their creditor. Perhaps in the long run that will be true. Maybe, thanks to Stendhal, we shall transcend Stendhal. But that will be because he has ceased to speak to us, because his writings have lost their power of expression for us. As long as language is functioning authentically, it is not a simple invitation to the listener or reader to discover in himself significations that were already there. It is rather the trick whereby the writer or orator, touching on these significations already present in us, makes them yield strange sounds. At first these sounds seem false or dissonant. However, because the writer is so successful in converting us to his system of harmony, we adopt it henceforth as our own. From then on, between the writer and ourselves there remain only the pure relations of spirit to spirit. Yet all this began through the complicity of speech and its echo, or to use Husserl's lively phrase referring to the perception of others, through the "coupling" of language.

Reading is an encounter between the glorious and impalpable incarnations of my own speech and the author's speech. As we have said, reading projects us beyond our own thoughts toward the other person's intention and meaning, just as perception takes us to things themselves across a perspective of which we become aware only after the event. But my power of transcending myself through reading is mine by virtue of my being a speaking subject capable of linguistic gesticulation, just as my perception is possible only through my body. The patch of light which falls at a different point on each of my retinas is seen by me as a single distant spot, because I possess sight and a mobile body which confront external messages with a viewpoint in which the spectacle is organized, arrayed, and equilibrated. Similarly, I cut straight through the scribbling to the book, because I have built up in myself a strange expressive organism which can not only interpret the conventional meaning of the book's words and techniques but can even allow itself to be transformed and endowed with new organs by the book. One can have no idea of the power of language until one has taken stock of that working or constitutive language which emerges when the constituted language, suddenly off center and out of equilibrium, reorganizes itself to teach the reader—and even the author—what he never knew how to think or say. Language leads us to the things themselves to the precise extent that it *is* signification before *having* a signification. If we concede language only its secondary function, it is because we presuppose the first as given, because we make language depend upon an awareness of truth when it is actually the vehicle of truth. In this way we are putting language before language.

We shall attempt elsewhere to develop these remarks more fully in a theory of expression and truth.[5] It will be necessary then to clarify or explicate the experience of speech in terms of what we know from the sciences of psychology, behavior dis-

5. TRANSLATOR: For references to Merleau-Ponty's projected writings, see "An Unpublished Text by Maurice Merleau-Ponty: A Prospectus of His Work," trans. Arleen B. Dallery, in *The Primacy of Perception*, ed. James M. Edie (Evanston: Northwestern University Press, 1964).

orders, and linguistics. It will also be necessary to consider those philosophical positions which claim to resolve the problem of expression by treating it as a species among the pure acts of signification which philosophical reflection makes perfectly clear to us. But that is not our task at present. We simply mean to initiate such a study by trying to illustrate the function of expression in literature, reserving a more complete explanation for another work. However, it is, of course, unusual to begin a study of expression with, so to speak, its most complex function and to proceed from there to the simpler ones. We therefore must justify the procedure by making it clear that the phenomenon of expression, as it appears in literary speech, is no curiosity or introspective fantasy marginal to the philosophy or science of language. We must show that the phenomenon of expression belongs both to the scientific study of language and to that of literary experience, and that these two studies overlap. How could there be a division between the science of expression, provided it conceives its subject as broadly as it should, and the lived experience of expression, where it is lucid enough? Science is not devoted to another world but to our own; in the end it refers to the same things that we experience in living. Science constructs everyday objects by combining pure defined ideas the same way that Galileo constructed the fall of a body on an inclined plane from the ideal case of free fall. Ultimately, however, ideas are always subject to the constraint of illuminating the opacity of objects, and the theory of language must gain access to the experience of speaking subjects. The idea of a possible language is shaped upon and assumes the actual language which we speak and which we are. Linguistics is nothing but a rigorous and conceptual way of clarifying, in terms of all the other facts of language, the speech which declares itself in us and to which, even in the midst of our scientific work, we are still attached as if by an umbilical cord.

Some would like to break this tie and get away from the confused and annoying situation of a being who is what he is talking about. They would like to consider language and society as if they had never been caught up in it, to adopt a bird's-eye view or a divine understanding. In other words, they would like to be without a point of view. There are two ways, one Platonic and the other nominalist, of talking about a language without words —or at least in such a way that the significations of the words used, once redefined, never exceed what one invests in them and expects from them. The first is Husserl's "eidetic of language" or "pure grammar," which he outlined in his early writings; the other is a logic concerned only with the formal properties of significations and their rules of transformation. In the second view, those words or formulae which resist analysis by definition have no meaning for us; furthermore, no problem is raised by what is non-sense. A question is merely asked in the expectation of a yes or no, and in either case the result is a proposition. The proposal is to create a system of precise significations which would translate everything in a language that is clear and thus constitute a model to which language can add only error and confusion. Such a standard would provide a measure of any individual's power of expression. In the end the sign would function purely as an index, without any admixture of signification. But no one dreams any more of a logic of invention, and even those who think it is possible to express, by means of an arbitrary algorithm, every well-formed proposition do not believe that this purified language would exhaust everyday language any more than it could be absorbed by everyday language. For how should we attribute to non-sense everything in everyday language which goes beyond the definitions of the algorithm or of a "pure grammar," when it is precisely in this alleged chaos that new relations will be found which make it both necessary and possible to introduce new symbols?

Once the novelty has been integrated and order temporarily reestablished, there can be no question of making the system of pure logic and pure grammar self-subsistent. It is known that this system is always on the verge of signification. By itself it never signifies anything, since everything it expresses has been abstracted from a ready-made language and from an *omnitudo realitas* which in principle it cannot embrace. Reflection cannot close itself off from the significations it has recognized or make them the standard of meaning. It cannot treat speech and everyday language as simple instances of itself, because ultimately it is through them that the algorithm means something. At least one question is not merely a provisional form of the proposition, and it is this question which the algorithm tirelessly puts to factual thought. There is no special question about being for which there is not a corresponding yes or no in being which settles it. But the question of knowing why there are questions and how there come to be those nonbeings who do not know but would like to know cannot find a response in being.

Philosophy is not the passage from a confused world to a universe of closed significations. On the contrary, philosophy begins with the awareness of a world which consumes and destroys our established significations but also renews and purifies them. To say that self-sufficient thought always refers to a thought enmeshed in language is not to say that thought is alienated or that language cuts thought off from truth and certainty. We must understand that language is not an impediment to consciousness and that there is no difference, for consciousness, between self-transcendence and self-expression. In its live and creative state, language is the gesture of renewal and recovery which unites me with myself and others. We must learn to reflect on consciousness *in* the hazards of language and as quite impossible without its opposite.

In the "I speak," psychology rediscovers for us an operation, a dimension, and relations which do not belong to thought in the ordinary sense. "I think" means there is a certain locus called "I" where action and awareness of action are not different, where being confounds itself with its own awareness of itself, and thus where no intrusion from outside is even conceivable. Such an "I" could not *speak.* He who speaks enters into a system of relations which presuppose his presence and at the same time make him open and vulnerable. Certain sick people believe that someone else is talking inside their head or in their body, or that someone else is talking when it is they themselves who are pronouncing or at least mouthing the words. Whatever one's view of the relation between healthy and pathological behavior, speech must, in its normal functioning, be of such a nature that disorders in it are always possible. There must be something in the very heart of speech which makes it susceptible to these pathologies. If one says that a patient is experiencing bizarre or confused feelings in his body, or, as they say, "problems of coenesthesia," one is simply inventing an entity or phrase which, instead of explaining the problem, merely baptizes it. On closer inspection, the so-called problems of coenesthesia have widespread ramifications, and a change in them also involves a change in our relations with others. I am speaking and I think that it is my heart which is speaking; I am speaking and I think it is someone else speaking to me or in me, or even that someone knew before I said it what I was going to say—all these phenomena which are so often associated must have something in common. The psychologists discern the common factor in our relations with others. "The patient feels as though there is no boundary between himself and others. . . . This leads us to conclude that . . . strictly speaking . . . what is involved is the loss of the distinction between action and passivity, between the self and others." [6]

Speech defects are thus related to disturbances of the lived body and interpersonal relations. How are we to understand this relationship? It arises because speech and understanding are moments in the unified system of self-other. The substratum of this system is not a pure "I" (which would never see anything more than an object of its own reflection placed *before* itself), but rather an "I" endowed with a body which reveals its thoughts sometimes to attribute them to itself and at other times to impute them to someone else. I accommodate to the other person through my language and my body. Even the distance which the normal subject puts between himself and others, as well as the clear distinction between speaking and listening, are modalities of the system of embodied subjects. Verbal hallucination is another modality of the same system. The patient can believe that someone is speaking to him when in fact it is he himself speaking, because the principle underlying this aberration is part of the human situation. As an embodied subject I am exposed to the other person, just as he is to me, and I *identify* myself with the person speaking before me.

Speaking and listening, action and perception, are quite dis-

6. Henri Wallon, *Les Origines du caractère chez l'enfant* (Paris: Presses Universitaires de France, 1962), pp. 135–36.

tinct operations for me only when I reflect upon them. Then I analyze the spoken words into "motor impulses" or "articulated elements," understanding them as auditory "sensations and perceptions." When I am actually speaking I do not first *figure* the *movements* involved. My whole bodily system concentrates on finding and saying the word, in the same way that my hand moves toward what is offered to me. Furthermore, it is not even the word or phrase that I have in mind but the person. I speak to him as I find him, with a certainty that at times is prodigious. I use words and phrases he can understand or to which he can react. If I have any tact, my words are both a means of action and feeling; there are eyes at the tips of my fingers. When I am listening, it is not necessary that I have an *auditory perception* of the articulated sounds but that the conversation pronounces itself within me. It summons me and grips me; it envelops and inhabits me to the point that I cannot tell what comes from me and what from it.

Whether speaking or listening, I project myself into the other person, I introduce him into my own self. Our conversation resembles a struggle between two athletes in a tug-of-war. The speaking "I" abides in its body. Rather than imprisoning it, language is like a magic machine for transporting the "I" into the other person's perspective. "There is . . . in language a two-way action; one which is induced by our own presence and another which we bring about in the *socius* by regarding him as being outside ourselves."[7] Language continuously reminds me that the "incomparable monster" which I am when silent can, through speech, be brought into the presence of *another myself*, who re-creates every word I say and sustains me in reality as well. There can be speech (and in the end personality) only for an "I" which contains the germ of a depersonalization.* Speaking

7. Daniel Lagache, *Les Hallucinations verbales et la parole* (Paris: Presses Universitaires de France, 1934), p. 139.

* The synthesis of coupling or transition (the *socius* is not represented, but represented as representing) $\frac{\text{looking}}{\text{gesture}}, \frac{\text{listening}}{\text{speaking}}$. Listening and speaking, which begin as simple modalities of perception and movement, go beyond them through the structure of language, the creation of "signs." At two levels, the recognition of the passive by

and listening not only presuppose thought but—even more essential, for it is practically the foundation of thought—the capacity to allow oneself to be pulled down and rebuilt again by the other person before one, by others who may come along, and in principle by anyone. The same transcendence which we found in the literary uses of speech can also be found in everyday language. This transcendence arises the moment I refuse to content myself with the established language, which in effect is a way of silencing me, and as soon as I truly speak to someone. Formerly, psychologists regarded language as merely a series of images, a verbal hallucination, or a purely imaginary exuberance. Their critics regarded language as the simple product of a pure mental function. We now regard language as the reverberation of my relations with myself and with others.

It is natural, after all, that the psychologist's analysis of man's speech should emphasize the way we express ourselves in language. However, that does not prove that communication is the primary function of speech. If I am to communicate with another person, I must first have available a language which names the things he and I can see. The psychologist's analysis takes this primordial function for granted. The psychologist's account, as well as a writer's reflections, would very likely seem superficial if, instead of considering language as a medium of human relations, we looked at it as the expression of objects or

---

the active and of the active by the passive, of the person spoken to by the speaker, is projection and introjection. The study that I made of the whirlwind of language, of the other as a force drawing me toward a meaning, applies in the first place to the whirlwind of the other drawing me toward himself. It is not simply that I am *fixed* by the other, that he is the X by whom I am *seen*, frozen. He is the person spoken to, i.e., an offshoot of myself, outside, my double, my twin, because I make him do everything that I do and he makes me do the same. It is true that language is founded, as Sartre says, but not on an apperception; it is founded on the phenomenon of the mirror, ego–alter ego, or of the echo, in other words, of a carnal generality: what warms me, warms him; it is founded on the magical action of like upon like (the *warm* sun makes me *warm*), on the fusion of me embodied—and the world. This foundation does not prevent language from coming back dialectically over what preceded it and transforming the purely carnal and vital coexistence with the world and bodies into a coexistence of language.

in terms of its entire history apart from its everyday uses, as though we could survey it the way a linguist does. It is here that we encounter one of the paradoxes of science, namely, that science itself is the surest road to the speaking subject.

Let us take as a text the famous page from Valéry where he expresses so well what is overwhelming for the man whose thought is tied to history and to language.

> *What is reality?*, the philosopher asks; and *What is freedom?* He puts himself in a state of ignorance concerning the origins of these nouns, which are indistinguishably metaphorical, social, and statistical, so that as they slide toward the undefinable the philosopher can produce the most profound and delicate compositions according to his fancy. The philosopher would not be satisfied to find his question answered simply by the history of a word through the ages. For the detailed story of the mistakes, the figurative uses, the number of incoherent and peculiar locutions, through which a poor word becomes as complex and mysterious as an individual and arouses the same almost anxious curiosity as the life of an individual, conceals itself from any precise analysis. The word is an accidental creature with simple needs, an old makeshift invented in the mixing of peoples. Finally, it acquires the most noble destiny of arousing all the powers of interrogation and capacities for response in the wonderously attentive mind of the philosopher.[8]

It is quite true that thought first of all involves thought about words. But Valéry believed that words contain nothing but the sum of misunderstandings and misinterpretations which have brought them from their proper meaning to their figurative meaning. Thus he believed that man's philosophical questioning would cease once man took note of the hazards which have joined contradictory meanings to the same word. However, that is again conceding too much to rationalism. It amounts to stopping halfway on the road to an understanding of contingency. Behind his nominalism is an extreme confidence in knowledge. For Valéry at least believed in the possibility of a history of words capable of completely analyzing their meaning and eliminating the problem raised by the ambiguity of words as a false problem. Yet the

8. Paul Valéry, *Variété III* (Paris: Gallimard, 1936), pp. 176–77.

paradox is that, even though the history of language contains too many hazards to permit a logical development, it nevertheless produces nothing for which there is not a reason. Even when each word, according to the dictionary, has a great number of meanings, we go straight to the one which fits a given sentence (and if there remains some ambiguity, we find a further expression for it). Finally, there is the paradox that there is meaning for us, although we inherit words which are so worn and exposed by history to the most imperceptible changes of meaning. We speak and we understand one another, at least at the start. If we were enclosed in the contradictory meanings which words acquire historically, we would not even have the idea of speaking; the need for expression would be undermined. Thus language is not, while it is functioning, the simple product of the past it carries with it. The past history of language is the visible trace of a power of expression which that history in no way invalidates. Moreover, since we have abandoned the fantasy of a pure language or an algorithm concentrating in itself the power of expression and only lending it to historical languages, we must find in history itself, with all its disorder, that which nevertheless makes possible the phenomenon of communication and meaning.

The findings of the sciences of language are decisive here. Valéry restricted himself to the option of the philosopher who believes he can capture pure significations through reflection, and so he stumbled over the misinterpretations built up in the history of words. Today psychology and linguistics reveal that it is in fact possible to forsake a timeless philosophy without falling into irrationalism. Saussure shows admirably that if words and language in general, considered over time—or, as he says, diachronically—offer an example of virtually every semantic slippage, it cannot be the history of the word or language which determines its present meaning; for example, etymology cannot tell me what the contemporary meaning of *thought* is. Most speaking subjects are ignorant of etymology—or, rather, in its popular form, etymology is imaginary; it projects the present meaning of words into a fictional history which it does not explain but presupposes. Whatever the hazards and confusions in the path of the French language—and this reeling path can and should be reconstructed—it is still a fact that we speak and carry on dialogue, that the historical chaos of language is caught up in our determination to express ourselves and to understand those who are members of our linguistic community. In the present, or synchronically, contemporary usage is not reducible to the inevitable legacies of the past. Alongside the linguistics of *language,* which gives the impression, in the extreme, that language is a series of chaotic events, Saussure has inaugurated a linguistics of *speech,* which would reveal in it at each moment an order, a system, a totality without which communication and the linguistic community would be impossible.

Saussure's successors have even questioned whether he can simply juxtapose the synchronic and diachronic viewpoints. After all, each of the phases described by a longitudinal study has been a living moment of speech, stretched toward communication, and every past has been a present turned toward the future. Then, if the expressive exigencies of a synchronic moment and the equilibrium imposed by them could not be spread over a lapse of time, in order to define, at least for a phase of the diachronic movement, a certain sense of the probable transformations, or at least a provisory *law of equilibrium,* until that equilibrium, once attained, in turn would pose new problems that would tip the language over into a new cycle of development.* . . . In any case, Saussure has the great merit of having taken the step which liberates history from historicism and makes a new conception of reason possible. Even if every word, every form of language, taken separately, receives in the course of its history a series of discordant significations, there is nothing equivocal in the total language considered in each of its phases. The mutations in every signifying apparatus, however unexpected they may seem when taken singly, are integral with those of all the others, and that is what makes the whole remain a means of communication. *Objective* history was—as is all history, for Saussure—an analysis which decomposes language and in general institutions

* It is not necessary for the synchronic viewpoint to be instantaneous. As the overlap of each part of speech upon the whole, it must also be the overlap of one temporal phase upon another, an existential eternity.

and societies into an infinite number of accidents. But history cannot be our only approach to language, because language would then become a prison. It would determine even what one could say about it and, being always presupposed in what is said about it, it would be incapable of any clarification. Even the science of language, enveloped in its present state, would be unable to reach a truth of language, and thus objective history would destroy itself.*

In Saussure, it is precisely the envelopment of language by language which saves rationality, because this overlap is no longer comparable to the objective movement of the observer who compromises his observation of other movements. On the contrary, the envelopment attests to a permanent affinity between my speaking and the language about which I am speaking. There is an "I speak" which ends doubt about language in the same way that the "I think" terminated universal doubt. Everything I say about language presupposes it, but that does not invalidate what I say; it only shows that language is not an object, that it is capable of repetition, that it is accessible from the inside. If we were to consider today the languages of the past, supposing we were successful in recapturing the system of spoken words those languages had constituted in each of their historical stages, then, behind the undeniable circumstances that have modified them—the usury of forms, phonetic decadence, the contagion of other tongues, invasions, the practices of the court, the decisions of the academy—we would discover the coherent motivations through which these accidents have been incorporated into a self-maintaining system of expression. The history of language insofar as it is objective history leads to skepticism, because it makes each of its stages appear as a pure event and shuts itself up in the period when it was written. But this present suddenly reveals itself as presence to a system of expression and, at a stroke, all other presents too. Thus, behind events, there is sketched the series of systems that have always striven for expres-

* Saussure shows it is necessary that there be an interior of language, a thought distinct from the linguistic material, and yet tied to it, not "logical."

sion. The inalienable subjectivity of my speech enables me to understand those extinct subjectivities of which objective history gives me only traces. Since I speak and am able to learn from my exchange with other speaking subjects what the meaning is of a language, even the history of the language is then not just a series of events external to one another and external to us. Pure objectivity led to doubt. The radical awareness of subjectivity enables me to rediscover other subjectivities and thereby the truth of the linguistic past. The accidents of history have been absorbed internally by an intention to communicate which transforms them into a system of expression, and this they remain today in the effort I make to understand the past of the language. External history repeats itself in an internal history, which, from synchrony to synchrony, gives a common meaning to at least certain cycles of development. The recourse to speech, to lived language—this methodical subjectivism—annuls Valéry's "absurdism," which is the inevitable conclusion of knowledge as long as one considers subjectivity a mere residual, a conjunction of accidents, in other words, from the outside. The solution of the doubts concerning language is to be found, not in a recourse to any universal language hovering over history, but in what Husserl later calls the "living present," in a speech, the variant of all the languages that were spoken before me, as well as the model for me of what they were. . . .

It remains for us to understand the synchronic meaning of language. This demands a reversal of our habits. From the very fact that we are speaking we are led to think that our forms of expression coincide with the things themselves; thus in foreign speech we look for what is so well expressed by our own. Even the rigorous Husserl, at the beginning of his career, when postulating the principles of a "pure grammar," demanded that a table of the fundamental forms of language be drawn, after which it would be possible to determine "how German, Latin, Chinese express 'the' existence proposition, 'the' categorical proposition, 'the' hypothetical premise, 'the' plural, 'the' modalities of possibility, of probability, 'the' negative, etc." He adds that "one cannot ignore the problem of knowing whether the grammarian will satisfy himself with his personal and prescientific opinions upon the forms of signification, or with the empirical and confused examples that any historical grammar offers him, for example, Latin grammar—or if he has before his eyes the pure system of forms in a scientifically determined and theoretically coherent formulation—that is, that of our own theory of the forms of signification." [9] Husserl forgot only one thing—that to achieve a universal grammar it is not enough to leave Latin grammar, and that the list of the possible forms of signification which he gives bears the mark of the language which he himself spoke.

It always appears to us that the operations of experience codified in our language follow the very articulations of being, because it is through them that we relate to being. Wishing to think language, that is, to reduce it to the state of an object before thought, we always risk treating those operations through which our language tries to determine being as an intuition of the being of language. But what are we to say, when the science of language—which in truth is only a more varied experience of language extended to the speech of others—teaches us that it does not admit the categories of our language, and furthermore that they are a retrospective and inessential expression of our own power of speech? There is no grammatical analysis that can discover elements common to all languages. Neither does each language necessarily contain the modes of expression found in others. In Peul the negative is signified by intonation; [10] the dual in ancient Greek is confused with the plural in French; the aspect in Russian has no equivalent in French; and the form in Hebrew that is called the future is used to mark the narrative past, while the preterite form can be used for the future tense; Indo-European had no passive or infinitive; modern Greek and Bulgarian have

9. Husserl, *Logische Untersuchungen* (Halle: Niemeyer, 1913), II, 339; published in France as *Recherches logiques*, trans. H. Elie with L. Kelkel and R. Schérer (Paris: Presses Universitaires de France, 1959), II, 135–36. Husserl was later to take up repeatedly the problem of the relations between reason and history, to end, in his last writings, with a philosophy in which they are identified. [EDITOR: This unfinished note mentions only the *Origin of Geometry*.]

10. TRANSLATOR: The Peul are an African tribal people. See Pierre-Francis Lacroix, "Le Peul," in *Le Langage*, Encyclopédie de la Pléiade (Paris: Gallimard, 1968), p. 1068–89.

lost their infinitives—but still one cannot reduce to a system the modes of expression of even *one* language.[11] Confronted with living usage, lexical or grammatical significations are only approximations. It is impossible in French to mark where the semantemes or words finish, where the simple morphemes begin: the *quidi* of spoken language (*j'ai faim, qu'il dit*) began by being made out of words: now it is nothing more, in everyday use, than a morpheme. The pronoun and auxiliary in "*il a* fait" [he has done] began as semantemes; now they have no other value than the augment, the sigma [σ], and the word ending in the Greek aorist. "I," "you," "me," "thou," "it" began by being words and there are still cases where they are employed in isolation (I say *it*), but each time they appear joined to their verb, as in "I say, you say, he says" they are no more than the final *o* of the latín *dico* [I say] and can be treated as a sort of frontal inflection of the verb and have no more worth than semantemes. In French the gender of a word has hardly any existence apart from the definite article that supports it: in words which begin with a vowel and an elision hides the gender of the definite article, the gender of the word itself starts to float and can even change. In spoken language the active and passive are not the entities defined by grammarians, and the latter is almost never the inverse of the first. One can see it invade the active conjugation and wedge in a passive with the verb "to be" [*être*] which is hard to bring under the strict sense of the passive. The categories of noun, verb, and adjective themselves impinge upon one another. "A morphological system always contains only a restricted number of categories which impose themselves and are dominant. But in each system there are always other systems that introduce themselves and interweave. These systems represent, alongside the fully developed grammatical categories, other categories in the process of disappearing or, on the contrary, of taking shape." [12]

11. Joseph Vendryès, *Le Langage* (Paris: La Renaissance du livre, 1923), pp. 106–34. [TRANSLATOR: Later edition (Paris: Editions Albin, 1968), pp. 93 ff. Subsequent page numbers in brackets refer to this edition.]

12. *Ibid.*, p. 131 [p. 130]. (Exact text of the second sentence: "But in each system there are always more or fewer other systems.")

Now these facts of linguistic usage can be understood in two ways: one can continue to believe that all they involve are contaminations, disorders, accidents that nothing in this world can escape. Thus one retains, against all argument, the classical conception of expression according to which the clarity of language derives from the pure relation of denotation that can in principle be established between signs [?] and limpid significations. But then one risks missing what is an essential feature of expression. For without having made an ideal analysis of our language and despite the difficulties one would involve, we do understand one another in language as it is. Therefore, in the heart of the spirit, it is not analysis which makes communication possible. At every moment, beneath the system of official grammar which attributes a given signification to each sign, one can see another expressive system emerge which is the vehicle of the signification but proceeds differently: *expression* in this case is not suited point by point to what is expressed; each element is not specific and obtains its linguistic existence only from what it receives from the others and the modulation it introduces to the rest of the system. It is the whole which possesses meaning, not each part. The particle ἄν in classical Greek is not only untranslatable in French, it is undefinable in Greek itself. With all the morphemes (and we have seen that the line between the semanteme and the morpheme is not clear) we are not dealing with words but with "coefficients," "exponents,"[13] or again, "linguistic tools" which have *use-value* rather than signification. Each by itself has no signifying power that one can isolate, and yet, when they are joined together in speech or, as it is called, the verbal chain, they all make unquestionable sense. The clarity of language is not behind it in a universal grammar we may carry upon our person; it is before language, in what the infinitesimal gestures of any scrawling on the paper or each vocal inflection reveals to the horizon as their meaning. For speech, understood in this way, the idea of a *finished expression* is chimerical: such an idea is what we call successful communication. But successful communication occurs only if the listener, instead of following the

13. *Ibid.*, p. 99 [p. 103].

verbal chain link by link, on his own account resumes the other's linguistic gesticulation and carries it further.*

It seems to us that the French "l'homme que j'aime" is a more complete expression than "the man I love." But Saussure makes the profound remark that this is because we speak French. It seems quite natural for us to say "Peter hits Paul," and the action of the one on the other is made explicit or expressed through the transitive verb. But again that is because we speak French. This construction is not in itself more expressive than any other. One could even say that it is less expressive, since the only morpheme which indicates the relation between Peter and Paul is, as Vendryès says, a zero morpheme.[14] "The man I love" is no less eloquent to the English. "From the sole fact that one understands a linguistic complex . . . this series of terms is the adequate expression of the thought."[15] Thus we must disabuse ourselves of the habit of "*under*standing" [*sous-entendre*] the relative pronoun in English. That is speaking French in English, it is not speaking English. Nothing is *under*stood in the English phrase, the moment it is comprehended—or rather, in any language at all there is nothing but *under*standings; the very ideas of a complete expression and of a signifier that would exactly cover the signified are both inconsistent.† It is not by depositing the *whole* of my thought in *words* from which it can be extracted by others that I communicate with them. With my throat, my voice, my intonation, and, of course, with the words, with my preferred constructions and the time I allow each part of the phrase, I com-

* The "clarity" of language is of a perceptual order.

14. *Ibid.*, p. 93 [p. 96].

15. Ferdinand de Saussure, *Cours de linguistique générale* (Paris: Payot, 1949), p. 197. [English translation by Wade Baskin, *Course in General Linguistics*, ed. Charles Bally and Albert Sechehaye with Albert Reidlinger (New York: Philosophical Library, 1959).]

† Communication at the preobjective level. Signification is a quasi-sensorial carry-over: it is a contour in the linguistic universe. That is how a word can be an insult, an "intelligible mouthful." Each spoken phrase must be understood not as a "perception," but as a gesture that will reach a cultural whole. (That is the source of the relative indifference of signs toward each other: they are only diacritical.)

pose an enigma that has only one solution such that the other person, silently accompanying this melody bristling with changes, with switches and falls, can manage to take it into his own repertoire and say it with me, and this is what it means to understand. Vendryès makes a profound observation: "To make the reader feel the contrary of a given impression, it is not enough to bracket the words which convey it with a negative. For that is not the way to suppress the impression one wishes to avoid: one evokes the image, while thinking he is banishing it. . . . The grammatical morpheme should not be confused with what may be called the 'expressive' morpheme." [16] There are denials that affirm. The meaning is beyond the letter, the meaning is always ironic. In cases where what is expressed seems to us to have been caught, directly or prosaically, where grammar operates more than style, it is only because the gesture is habitual, our repetition is immediate, and no shifting around of our ordinary operations is required. The cases where, on the contrary, we have to find in the phrase as it occurs the rule of equivalences and substitutions it involves, to find the right key to the language, the meaning of the verbal chain—these cases are the very ones by which we understand the most ordinary facts of language.

Thus there is a primary reflection through which I redeem the signification of signs but which evokes a second reflection this side of that distinction in which I rediscover the effective operation of speech.

Even what I call signification appears to me as thought without any admixture of language only through the power of language to carry me toward what is expressed; and what I call a sign, reducing it to an inanimate envelope or an external manifestation of thought, approaches as closely as possible to signification as soon as I consider the way it functions in living language. "The meaning of things (*die Meinung*) is not found outside of words, or next to them; but through speech (*redend*) I constantly fulfill an act of internal sense, which blends with the words and, so to speak, animates them. The result of this animation is that the words and all speech incarnate meaning in themselves and

16. Vendryès, *Langage*, pp. 159–60 [p. 154].

carry it, embodied in themselves, as meaning."[17] Before language carries the significations which hide as much as reveal its operations, and which, once born, will appear to be simply coordinate with the inert signs, it must secrete through its internal organization a certain originary sense upon which the significations will be outlined. There must be a study which places itself above institutionalized language, which considers the modulations introduced by speech, the verbal chain, as expressive in themselves,[18] and which clarifies, this side of all established nomenclature, the "linguistic value" immanent in the acts of speech.

This primordial level of language may be approached by defining signs, as Saussure does, not as the representations of certain significations but as the means of differentiation in the verbal chain and of "oppositive, relative and negative entities" in speech.[19] A language is less a sum of signs (words, grammatical and syntactical forms) than a methodical means of differentiating signs from one another and thereby constructing a linguistic universe of which we later say—once it is precise enough to crystallize a significative intention and to have it reborn in another—that it expresses a world of thought, as it gives it its existence in the world and only takes away "a little of the renewable action and independent existence from the transitive character of internal phenomena."[20] "In language, there are only differences without positive terms. Whether one takes the signified or the signifying, language contains neither ideas nor sounds that could preexist before the linguistic system, but only conceptual differences and phonic differences which result from this system."[21]

17. Husserl, *Formale und transzendentale Logik* (Halle: Niemeyer, 1929), p. 20. Husserl's text is as follows: "Diese (die Meinung) aber liegt nicht äusserlich neben den Worten; sondern redend vollziehen wir fortlaufend ein inneres, sich mit Worten verschmelzendes, sie gleichsam beseelendes Meinen. Der Erfolg dieser Beseelung ist, dass die Worte und die ganzen Reden in sich eine Meinung gleichsam verleiblichen und verleiblicht in sich als Sinn tragen."
18. Phonology is such a study.
19. Saussure, *Cours*, p. 171.
20. Valéry.
21. Saussure, *Cours*, p. 172.

French is not the words for sun, or the word for shadow, or the word for earth, any more than an indefinite number of words and phrases, each endowed with its own sense—French is the configuration that all these words and phrases draw according to their use in the French language. This would be strikingly apparent if we did not yet know the words' meaning and were limited like a child to repeating their coming and going, their recurrence, the way they associate with one another, evoke or repel one another, and together make up a melody with a definite style.

It is frequently observed that it is impossible at any given moment to make an inventory of a vocabulary—whether of a child, of an individual, or of a language. Should one count as distinct words those that are formed mechanically from the same original word? Does one include a word that is still understood but hardly used and marginal to everyday use? Like the visual field, an individual's linguistic field ends in vagueness, because speaking is not having at one's disposal a certain number of signs. Speaking is possessing language as a principle of distinction, whatever number of signs it permits us to specify. There are languages in which one cannot say "to sit in the sun," [22] because they use particular words to refer to the rays of sunlight and keep the word "sun" for the star itself. In other words, the linguistic value of each word is defined only through the presence or absence of the words surrounding it. Since one can say the same thing in turn of those words, it seems that *language never says anything; it invents a series of gestures, which between them present differences clear enough for the conduct of language, to the degree that it repeats* itself, recovers and affirms itself, and purveys to *us the palpable flow and contours of a universe of meaning.* Moreover, the words and very forms for an analysis of this kind soon appear to be secondary realities, the results of a more originary differentiation. The syllables and letters, the turns of phrase, and the word endings are the sediments of a primary differentiation which, this time, precedes without any doubt the relation of sign to signification, since it is what makes the very

22. *Ibid.*, p. 167.

distinction between signs possible. The phonemes, too, which are the real foundations of speech, since they are reached through the analysis of spoken language and have no official existence in grammar and dictionaries, by themselves *mean nothing* one can specify. But for this very reason, they represent the originary form of signifying. They bring us into the presence of that primary operation, beneath institutionalized language, that creates the simultaneous possibility of significations and discrete signs. Like language itself, phonemes constitute a system, in other words, they are less a finite number of tools than a typical manner of modulation, an inexhaustible power of differentiating one linguistic gesture from another. Finally, to the extent that the differences are more precise, more systematic, phonemes appear in situations which themselves are better articulated and suggest even more that the whole process obeys an internal order, the power of revealing to the child what the adult had in mind.

Perhaps one can see better how language signifies, if one looks at it in the moment where it invents a means of expression. It is known that in French the accent is always on the last syllable except in words which end with a mute *e*, and that in Latin the accent is always on the penultimate syllable when it is long (*amīcus*) or on the preceding syllable if the penultimate is short (*ānima*). The system of inflections in Latin obviously could not survive unless the word endings remained perceptible. But, precisely because they were not accented, they became weak. At first language tried to *repair* them, by grafting onto French words the Latin endings that had remained more alive: hence the endings *ons* and *ez* in the first two persons plural; and certain past participles in *u* derived from Latin endings in *utus*, which are quite rare (*lu, vu, tenu, rompu*).[23] This was not enough; the decadence still continued. A moment was reached when what was in ruins became a model, and the disappearance of Latin endings which was produced by decadence was perceived by speaking subjects as the expression of a new principle. There is a period when the Latin accent, remaining on the syllable where it has always been, nevertheless changes its place through the

23. Vendryès, *Langage*, p. 195 [p. 185].

disappearance of the following syllables. "The position of the accent has changed without its having been touched." [24] The accent on the last syllable was then kept as a *rule,* since it encroached even upon borrowed words which owed nothing to Latin, or upon words which derived from it only through writing (facile, consul, ticket, burgrave).[25] With this sort of decision in the language, it became necessary to have a system that was no longer founded upon inflection but upon the generalized use of the preposition and article. Language then seized upon words which had been full and emptied them to make prepositions out of them (for example, *chez, casa, pendant, vu, excepté, malgré, sauf, plein*).[26]

How are we to understand this fruitful moment of language in which an accident is transformed into a reason and there suddenly arises, from a mode of speech that is becoming extinct, a new, more effective and expressive mode—in the way the ebb of the sea after a wave excites and enlarges the next wave? The way it happens is too indecisive for one to imagine some spirit of language or some decree on the part of speaking subjects that may be responsible for it. But it is also too systematic and presupposes too much connivance between different detailed facts for one to be able to reduce it to a sum of partial changes. The event has an interior, even though it is not the interior of a concept. "The system is never modified directly; in itself, it is unchangeable, only certain elements are changed without regard for the solidarity that binds them to the whole. It is as though one of the planets gravitating around the sun were to change in dimension and weight: this isolated fact would generate general consequences and displace the equilibrium of the entire solar system." [27] We need add simply that the new equilibrium of the solar system would be only the result of the action exerted by and upon each of its parts and that its results could be less rich,

24. Saussure, *Cours,* p. 126.
25. *Ibid.,* p. 127.
26. Vendryès, *Langage,* pp. 195–96 [p. 186]. [TRANSLATOR: "At (someone's house)," *casa,* "while," "considering," "except," "despite," "but," "full."]
27. Saussure, *Cours,* p. 125.

less productive, and, so to speak, of lesser quality than that which preceded it. On the contrary, the modes of expression in French which have taken the place of those from Latin have had the effect of reestablishing a power of expression which was threatened. What sustains the invention of a new system of expression, therefore, is the drive of speaking subjects who wish to be understood and who take over as a new mode of speaking the debris produced by another mode of expression.

Language is completely accidental and completely rational, because there is no expressive system that follows a plan or does not have its origin in some particular accident. Likewise, no accident becomes a linguistic instrument unless language breathes into it the value of a new mode of speech, by treating it as an example of a "rule" that in the future will apply to a whole sector of signs. We should not even place the fortuitous and the rational in two [?] distinct orders, as though men were the bearers of order and events were disorder. The will to expression itself is ambiguous and contains a ferment that works at modifying it. Every language, as Vendryès among others says, is subject at each moment to the twin but contrary demands of expressivity and uniformity.[28] For a mode of speech to be understood, it must be a matter of course; it must be generally accepted. This ultimately presupposes that a mode of speech has its analogue in other forms of speech based on the same pattern. But at the same time it should not be habitual to the point of becoming indistinguishable. It must still strike someone who hears it used, and its whole power of expression derives from its *not* being identical with its competitors.

To express oneself is, therefore, a paradoxical enterprise, since it presupposes that there is a fund of kindred expressions, already established and thoroughly evident, and that from this fund the form used should detach itself and remain new enough to arouse attention. It is an operation which tends toward its own destruction, since it suppresses itself to the extent that it ingratiates itself and annuls itself if it fails to do so. For this reason, one cannot conceive of an expression that could be definitive,

28. Vendryès, *Langage*, p. 192 [p.184].

since the very virtues that would make it general would simultaneously make it inadequate. As soon as speech gets hold of it, as soon as it comes *alive,* the best-reasoned artificial language becomes irregular and full of exceptions.[29] Languages are so sensitive to the interventions of general history and to their own usury only because they are secretly starved for changes that give them means of making themselves expressive once again.* Thus there is indeed an interior of language, a signifying intention which animates linguistic events and, at each moment, makes language a system capable of its own self-recovery and self-confirmation. But this intention exhausts itself to the extent that it is fulfilled. For its aim to be realized, it must not be completely realized, and for something to be said, it must not be said absolutely.

The expressive power of a sign derives from its part in a system and its coexistence with other signs and not from the possibility it may have been instituted by God or by nature to designate a signification. Moreover, even the sense of a language or the value of its current use, and the effective law of the system which is the ground of signification, are not first of all grasped by thinking subjects. They are practiced by speaking subjects and are present only in historical accidents which first suggested their significations and then become the *examples* for grammarians, in the way that a man's character is present in his gestures and his handwriting, apart from any psychology, or the way the geometrical definition of a circle is present in my view of its circular physiognomy. The signification of signs derives initially from their configuration in current usage, from the style of human relations that emanate from them, and only the blind and involuntary logic of things perceived, totally suspended in our body's activity, could lead us to a glimpse of the anonymous spirit

29. *Ibid.*, p. 193 [p. 184].

* Essential point: do not make synchrony instantaneous, because that would rest the "totality" of speech on the absolute, transcendent powers of "consciousness." There has to be a nonthetic ground of language in its immediately interior state, accident and reason must unite, each present must be differentiation in relation to the precedent. It is too much to say that there is no trace of the distant past in the present: if not consciousness of this past, there is at least consciousness of the past in general, of a historical type.

which, in the heart of language, invents a new mode of expression. Things perceived would not be evident for us and present in flesh and blood if they were not inexhaustible, never entirely given. They would not have the air of eternity we find in them unless they were open to an inspection that no time could terminate. In the same way, expression is never absolutely expression, what is expressed is never completely expressed. It is as essential to language that the logic of its construction never be of a kind that can be put into concepts as it is to truth never to be possessed, but only transparent through the clouded logic of a system of expression which bears the traces of another past and the seeds of another future.*

We must be sure to understand that all this does not invalidate the fact of expression and proves nothing against the truth of what is expressed. By invoking the sciences of language, we are not closing ourselves in a psychology or history of expression which could grasp only its present manifestations and would be blind toward the power which makes them possible, indeed, toward a true philosophy, which engenders and constitutes language as *one of the objects* of thought.† The progress of psy-

* All this only makes more clear the transcendence of signification in relation to language. Just as the analysis of perception makes clear the transcendence of the thing in relation to the contents and *Abschattungen*. The thing emerges over there, while I think I am grasping it in a given variation of the *hylē* where it is only in adumbration. Similarly, thought arises over there, while I am looking for it in a particular inflection of the verbal chain. But the power of transcendence in speech and perception derives precisely from their own organization. The transition to *Bedeutung* is not a leap into the "spiritual."

† [Against Vendryès: no limits to language, no structure of language (since system there is always mixed with other systems), no comparison between them, they all express equally well (refusal of values in Vendryès—perhaps Saussure). These limits and values exist; quite simply, they are of a perceptual order: there is a *Gestalt* of language, in the living present there is something of the expressed and nonexpressed; there is work to do. In the end language must signify something and not always be language about language. But signification and the sign belong to the perceptual order, not to the order of absolute spirit. Yes, there is a problem of knowing how the first signs became capable of sedimentation and of a whole (?) of culture; and there is a problem of knowing how to think the pre-

chology and linguistics consists precisely in that, by revealing the *speaking subject* and speech in the present, they manage to ignore the alternatives of the existing and possible, of the constituted and the constituting, of facts and the conditions of possibility, of contingency and reason, of science and philosophy. Indeed, while I am speaking, I do, of course, say *something*, and I rightly claim to go from the things said to the things themselves. It is with similar right that, over and above all the half-silences or all the *under*standings of speech, I claim to make myself understood and to introduce a difference between what has been said and what has never been said. Finally, it is with good right that I work at expressing myself, even if it is the nature of the means of expression to be transitory: for the moment, at least, I have said something, and Mallarmé's quasi silence is still something that has been expressed. What is always a jumble in every language, preventing it from being the reflection of some universal language—in which the sign would be the exact repetition of the concept—does not prevent language, in the living exercise of speaking, from fulfilling its role of revelation or from containing its typical evidences, its experiences of communication.

We are sufficiently convinced that language has a metaphysical significance—in other words, that it attests other relations and other properties than those which, according to common opinion, belong to the multiplicity of the things of nature, chained to a causality—by the experience of living language, since it characterizes as a comprehensible system and order that very speech which, considered from outside, is a conjunction of fortuitous events. In this regard, it is possible that linguistics has not always

---

sumptive fulfillment of language in nonlanguage, in thought. But these two facts are nothing else than the very fact of perception and rationality; of the logos of the aesthetic world. To ask for an explanation is (?) *obscurum per obscurius*.]

EDITOR: Another note is added to this: Sedimentation: the fact of the *Stiftung* of a meaning which will be *nachvollsichtbar*. Expressivity is temporary. But one will be able to return to the present in the past. There is a repetition of another past by my present. Each act of speech repeats all the others, that is why there are no absolute limits between languages. Sedimentation and reactivation.

realized to what extent its own findings remove us from positivism. The grammatical categories of sounds, forms, and words prove to be abstract, and each sort of sign in language as it exists functions only through the support of all the others. Nothing enables us to trace precise frontiers between dialects and languages, or between simultaneous and successive languages, and each of them is only "in reality a force that does not culminate in the act." [30] What we call the kinship of languages expresses much less the analogies of internal structure than a historical transition from one language to another altered by chance, though it could not have been shown without the very inquiry of the language substituting for it.[31] Thus the difficulties one finds in giving a rational formula to each language, of defining it unequivocally by an essence in which its characteristics would find their common *raison d'être*, and of establishing clear relations of derivation between these essences, far from authorizing us to pulverize language into a sum of fortuitously united facts and treating the very function of language as a void entity, in a sense would show that in this immense history, where nothing ends or begins suddenly, in this endless proliferation of aberrant forms, in this perpetual movement of languages where past, present, and future are mixed, no rigorous break is possible, and that, finally, there is only, strictly speaking, a single language in development.[32] *

If we abandon the abstract universality of a rational grammar which could contain the common essence of all languages, we would only rediscover the concrete universality of language,

30. Vendryès, *Langage*, p. 285 [p. 269].

31. *Ibid.*, p. 363 [p. 336]: "If we knew French only in its condition as a spoken language and in its present form, if we were also ignorant of other romance languages and Latin, it would not be so easy to prove French is an Indo-European language: some details of structure, such as the opposition of *il est, ils sont* (pronounced ilè, ison), or better still the forms of nouns of quantity or of personal pronouns, with some facts of vocabulary such as nouns of kind, that would be all French retained from Indo-European. Who knows if one could not find more topical reasons for relating it to Semitic or Finno-Hungarian?"

32. *Ibid.*, p. 273 [p. 259].

* Existential universal, existential eternity.

which can be different from itself without openly denying itself. Because I am speaking right now, my language is not a sum of facts for me but the only instrument there is for the will to be totally expressive. And *because it is so for me I am capable of entering into other systems of expression*, by understanding them at first as variants of my own system and then allowing myself to be inhabited by them to the point of thinking of my own language as a variant of theirs. The unity of language, the distinction among languages, their kinship, all cease to be unthinkable in modern linguistics, once one has given up the conception of an essence of languages and of language. They are simply to be conceived as a dimension which is neither that of the concept nor of essence, but of existence. Even if French is all cluttered with forms, words, and sounds that no longer exist, and others that are not yet canonical French, it is still true that the speaking subject is conscious of a norm of expression and very sensitive to unusual forms of speech. It is still true that, in the transition from Latin to French—even though there is no frontier that *one passes*—a moment comes when the frontier has definitely been passed. Also, comparisons of languages and the objective estimation of their expressive power are still possible, even though each one, in virtue of having been spoken, has *to a certain point* satisfied the need for expression. Even though no expression is ever absolute expression—rather, for that very reason—there are words which say things one way, others another way, and some that say more and others that say less. Although we cannot dream of a language which would reveal to us pure significations, and though no speech completely effaces itself before the meaning toward which it points—or for just that reason—there is still, in the exercise of language, the consciousness of saying something, the presumption of a fulfillment of language, a word which ends everything.

Simply, the distinct existence of systems of speech and of the significations which they intend belongs to the order of perception or of the present, and not to the order of the idea or the eternal. I cannot say precisely when the light of the setting sun turns from white to pink, but there is a moment when I see things pink in its light. I cannot say just when the image falling on the screen can be called a face, but there is a moment when there is a face there. If, in order to believe in the chair before me, I waited until I have verified that it meets all the criteria of a real chair, I would never be finished. Perception proceeds ahead of the criteria of thought and tells me what these appearances mean: a chair. Similarly, although nothing is ever said before universal history, there comes a day where all the signs that books and others made to me mean something and I understand it. If I were to suppose that they only called my attention to the pure signification which I already bore within me and which now comes to recover and, as it were, reabsorb the approximate expressions of it that were offered to me, then I would be renouncing the understanding of what it is to understand. For the power of language does not reside in the tête-à-tête it conducts between our spirit and things or, for that matter, in the privilege which might have been laid upon the first words of designating the very elements of being, as though all future knowledge and all later speech were limited to the combination of these elements. The power of language lies neither in that future of knowledge toward which it moves nor in that mythical past from which it has emerged: it lies entirely in its present, insofar as it succeeds in ordering the would-be key words to make them say more than they have ever said, and transcends itself as a product of the past, thus giving us the illusion of going beyond all speech to things themselves, because in effect we go beyond all given language. In that moment, something has been gained once and for all, founded forever, and it can be transmitted the way past acts of expression have been, not because we have grasped a piece of the intelligible world or rejoined adequate thought, but because our present use of language will be repeatable as long as the same language is in use or scientists are capable of restoring it to the present. The marvel that a finite number of signs, forms, and words should give rise to an indefinite number of uses, or that other and identical marvel that linguistic meaning directs toward something beyond language, is the very prodigy of speech, and anyone who tries to explain it in terms of its "beginning" or its "end" would lose sight of its "doing." In the living exercise of speech there is really a repetition of all preceding experience, an appeal to the fulfillment of language, a presumptive eternity. But this appeal is made the way the perceived object gives us the experience of being in the very moment that it sketches, in the evidence of the present, the outline of an experience and the presumption of an endless future that would confirm it. . . .

In sum, we have found that signs, morphemes, and words, taken one by one, signify nothing; they succeed in conveying signification only through their assembly, just as communication passes from the whole of spoken language to the whole of understood language. Speaking is spelling out at each point a communication whose principle is already established. It may be asked how this is possible, since, if what we are told of the history of the earth is well founded, speech must have had a beginning, and it begins again with each child. That the child proceeds to the whole from the parts of language—even if he uses only, to begin, some of its possibilities—is not surprising, since the functioning of adult speech offers itself to him as a model. At first he grasps it as a vague ensemble, and by a back-and-forth movement each of the instruments of expression which emerges from it sets off changes in the ensemble. But what can we say about the first speech of mankind? It could not rest upon an already established language; all we can say is that it had to be signifying of itself. But that is forgetting that the principle of communication had already been given in the fact that man perceives another man in the world as a part of the spectacle, and thus everything the other does already has the same sense as what I do, because his action (inasmuch as I am the spectator of it) is aimed at the same objects with which I deal. The first speech was not established in a world without communication, since it emerged from forms of conduct that were already common and took root in a sensible world which had already ceased to be a private world.* To be sure, speech brought to this primordial and mute communication as much and more than it received from it. Like all institutions, speech transformed what was congeneric in man. Speech inaugurated a new world. We who are inside it, and know what a Copernican revolution it introduced, may

* Logos of the aesthetic world and logos.

legitimately reject the perspectives which present the world of institutions and language as secondary and derivative with respect to the world of nature and live in a kind of religion of man. Yet, like all religions, this one lives only by borrowing from outside. It would lose consciousness of itself if it were to shut itself up in itself, and it would cease to honor man if it did not also know the silence that is prehuman. The first speech found its meaning in the context of already common forms of conduct, just as the first constitution continued while nevertheless transcending a spontaneous history. Since one cannot study the exchange processes, in the functioning of established language, through which the listener or reader goes beyond the linguistic gestures to their meaning, the mystery of the first speech is no greater than the mystery of all successful expression. In the one as in the other, a private spectacle is invaded by an agile meaning, indifferent to the individual darkness it comes to inhabit. But this void of meaning is prepared, like the whirl in a body of water, in the fullness of the individual life as soon as the sensible has coagulated into things. In a sense, speech repeats and goes beyond, but in a sense it conserves and continues, sense-certainty; it never quite pierces the "eternal silence" of private subjectivity. Even more, speech continues beneath the words and never ceases to envelop them, and, if ever voices were distant or unclear, or the language quite different from our own, we would be able, on meeting it, to rediscover the stupor of the first witness of the first speech.

We must pay a price for understanding language. To say that no sign signifies by itself, that language always refers back to language because at any moment only a few signs are received, is also to say that language is expressive as much through what is *between* the words as through the words themselves, and through what it does not say as much as what it says; just as the painter paints as much by what he traces, by the blanks he leaves, or by the brush marks that he does not make.* The act

* Analyze—what is the meaning of this reference to the *ordinary*, to the norm? There is here a typicality of communication which must be understood if one wants to understand the *Abweichungen* [TRANSLATOR: the deviations.]

of painting has two sides: there is the spot of color or stroke of charcoal one puts on the canvas or paper, and there is the effect of this spot on the whole, an effect that is quite incommensurate with the spot, since the latter is practically nothing and yet is enough to change a portrait or a landscape. Anyone observing the painter too closely, with his nose on the brush, would see only the reverse side of his work. The other side is this thin stroke of black, the place is the great sun spot that he begins to circumscribe. The experience has been tried: a camera has registered the work of Matisse in slow motion. The impression was overwhelming—to the point that, they say, Matisse himself was moved by it. The same brush which, to the eye, did not jump from one movement to another, could be seen meditating, in a suspended and solemn time, in an imminence, like the beginning of the world, beginning ten possible movements, performing in front of the canvas a sort of propitiatory dance, coming so close several times as almost to touch it, and finally coming down like lightning in the only stroke necessary.

There is, of course, something artificial in this analysis, and if at the end of the film Matisse believes that he really chose, on that particular day, between those possible strokes and, like Leibniz's God, solved an immense problem of minimum and maximum,* he is mistaken. He is not a demiurge, he is a man. In his mind's eye, he did not have all the possible gestures, he did not have to eliminate all but one of them, in order to make his choice rational. The camera and the slow motion make all the possibilities explicit. Matisse, settled in a man's time and vision, looked at the actual and virtual ensemble of his canvas and moved his hand toward the area which called for his brush so that the painting could be what it became in the end. He solved with a simple gesture the problem which, on analysis and reflection, seemed to contain an infinite number of givens,† just

* Minimum and maximum: defined within what limits?

† Compare the analysis of style below with miniatures. Style as preconceptual generality—generality of the "axis" which is preobjective and creates the *reality* of the world; the thing is there where I touch it; it is not a geometric of *Abschattungen;* it escapes *Erlebnisanalyse* (its "entrance" in its register is only [noted?] in my history)

as, according to Bergson, a hand in iron filings suddenly sets up a complicated pattern. Everything has occurred in the human world of perception and gesture, and it is the trick of the camera and the slow motion to give us a fascinating version of the events, making us believe Matisse's hand miraculously passed from the physical world, where infinite numbers of solutions are possible, to the world of perception and gesture, where only some are possible. Nevertheless, it is true that the hand hesitated, that it mediated. It is therefore true that there was a choice, that the stroke was chosen so as to satisfy ten conditions scattered on the painting, unformulated and unformulable for anyone other than Matisse, since they were defined and imposed only by the intention to make *this particular painting which did not yet exist.*

It is not different in the case of truly expressive speech—and thus of all language in its period of becoming established. Speech does not choose only one sign for one already defined signification, the way one searches for a hammer to drive in a nail or pincers to pull one out. It gropes around an intention to signify which has at its disposal no text to guide it, for it is just being written. And if we want to grasp speech in its most authentic operation in order to do it full justice, we must evoke all those words that could have come in its place that have been omitted; to feel the different way they would have impinged on and rattled the chain of language, to know at what point this particular speech was the only one possible * if this signification was to come into the world. . . . In brief, we should consider speech

---

because there is a transtemporality which is not that of the *ideal* but that of the deepest wound, incurable. This nonconstituted rationality of the thing-axis (a nonconstituted rationality is possible only if the thing is nonfrontal, ob-ject, but what bites into me, and what I bite into through my body; if the thing is, itself too, given through an indirect grasp, lateral like the other person—such a rationality has *decentering as the ground of meaning*) is already the analogue of the act of painting: one resolves problems not posed, i.e., what one does has more meaning than one knows. It is upon this primordial institution of the body that is founded the whole of symbolic elaboration, which itself consists in stepping evenly into an unknown domain.

* Notion of the possible: arbitrary, nonappearance, ex nihilo—but lateral appearance of an apparatus of meaning which uses its content only bit by bit.

before it has been pronounced, against the ground of the silence which precedes it, which never ceases to accompany it, and without which it would say nothing. Moreover, we should be sensitive to the thread of silence from which the tissue of speech is woven.* In expressions already habitual, there is a direct meaning which corresponds point by point to the established phrases, forms, and words. Precisely because these expressions are habitual, the gaps and element of silence are obliterated. However, the meaning of expressions in the process of becoming habitual can in principle be, as it were, a lateral or oblique meaning which results from the commerce between the words themselves (or from the available significations). It is a new way of shaking up the apparatus of language or of narrative to make it yield goodness knows what—precisely because what is said then has never before been said. If we want to understand language in its original mode of signifying, we shall have to pretend never to have spoken. We must perform a reduction upon language, without which it would still be hidden from our view—leading us back to what it signifies. We should look at language the way deaf people look at those who are speaking. We should compare the art of language with other arts of expression which do not have recourse to language and try to see language as one of these mute arts. It is possible that the meaning of language has certain privileges over the meaning of painting, and that in the end we must move beyond this parallel. But it is only by trying to do so that we can see what makes the comparison with painting ultimately unworkable and thereby have the chance of discovering what is peculiar to language.

* One does not know what one is saying, one knows after one has said it.

3 / The Indirect Language

EVEN IF WE MUST REFRAIN finally from treating painting as a language—which is one of the commonplaces of our time—and just test this platitude, we should have to start by recognizing that the parallel is in principle legitimate. Given that there are organisms, objects, or fragments of objects whose ponderous existence surrounds him, each one in its place, and yet all run through and intertwined on the surface by a network of vectors and a clustering of the lines of force to their roots, the painter throws away the fish and keeps the net. His look appropriates correspondences, questions, and answers which, in the world, are revealed only inaudibly and always smothered in the stupor of objects. He strips them, frees them, and looks for a more agile body for them.* Given, moreover, colors and a canvas which belong to the world, he suddenly deprives them of their inherence. The canvas, the very colors, by virtue of being chosen and composed in terms of some secret, to our sight cease to remain where they are; they make a hole in the plenum of the world. Like the fountains or the forests, they become the place where spirits appear. They are no longer there except as the minimum of matter that is needed for meaning to manifest itself.†

The task of language is similar. Given an experience, which

* "Metemsomatics" of art: what is transported?
† The imaginary is lodged in the world.

may be banal but for the writer captures a particular savor of life, given, in addition, words, forms, phrasing, syntax, even literary genres, modes of narrative that, through custom, are already endowed with a common meaning—the writer's task is to choose, assemble, wield, and torment these instruments in such a way that they induce the same sentiment of life that dwells in the writer at every moment, deployed henceforth in an imaginary world and in the transparent body of language. There is, then, on both sides, the same transmutation, the same migration of a meaning scattered in experience that leaves the flesh in which it did not manage to collect itself, mobilizes already capitalized instruments for its own profit, and employs them so that in the end they become the very body it had needed while in the process of acquiring the dignity of expressed meaning. Since the same expressive function is at work in both cases, it is possible to consider painting against the ground of language and language against the ground of painting. This must be done if we are to extract them from our prejudice, from the false evidence of what is a matter of course.

Our comparison between language and painting is possible only because of an idea of creative expression which is modern. However, for centuries painters and writers have worked without suspecting their common bond. Yet it is a fact, as André Malraux has shown, that each, in his own way and for his own reasons, has experienced the same adventure. Like language, painting at first lives in the milieu of the exterior holy. Paintings are acquainted with their own miracle only as an enigma, through the mirror of an exterior power. They make, from the transmutation of meaning into signification that is their function, a sacrifice to the Being whom they believe they are destined to serve. It is not enough to say that they offer themselves as the means of celebrating the sacrifice. That would not explain their universal and long indentification with religion. We must say that they themselves are a cult and a religion, because they have not assumed their own power. As long as art is devoted to the city and its gods, as long as speech is conceived as the simple exercise of a divinely instituted language, the prodigy of communication between men is projected behind us. Art and literature appear as the play in us of an art and speech whose origins contain everything in advance. It is from there that we must start to give its full meaning to the modern self-recovery of painting and language. For if we are very far from conceiving art and language as divine institutions of which we have only to make use, we are still full of the classical conception of art and language which is basically only a secularization of the divine conception of language—and which, indeed, is in many respects even less reconcilable with the modern awareness of expression. If art is the representation of a nature that it can at best embellish, but only by following the directions nature teaches it; if, as La Bruyère desired, our speech has no other role than to be the precise expression assigned in advance to each thought by a language of the things themselves, one may very well say that the art of painting and the art of writing are beginning to become autonomous, since they recognize no other master than truth or nature. But, in other respects, once detached from the sacred, that is, from what transcends man, and ruled according to a nature-in-itself, painting and writing cease to live in a state of tension. They become destined for a state of perfection in which complete expression is achieved, and it would require a real overthrow of received ideas for them to rediscover the awareness of their incompleteness. We ourselves are always tempted to return to this rationalism. We must therefore examine it more closely—with more tenacity than, perhaps, Malraux pursued it.

As Malraux says, everything shows that classical painting in Europe conceived itself as the representation of objects and men in their *natural* functioning. Consider the predilection for oil painting which, more than any other kind, allows the artist to attribute a distinct pictorial representation to each element of the object or the human face, or the search for signs which, when incorporated into the painting, would give the illusion of depth or volume through the play of light, foreshortening, or chiaroscuro—the research into movement, forms, tactile values, and different sorts of material (think of the patient studies which brought to perfection the representation of velvet). These secrets, these processes discovered by a painter and augmented by each generation, are elements of a general technique of representation which at the limit would reach the thing itself, man himself, which cannot be imagined for a moment to contain any accident or vagueness. They evoke a progress of painting toward a finished world and a complete man whose sovereign functioning it is the task of art to equal. Along this road whose end is clearly in view, one takes steps that need never be retraced. The career of a painter, the productions of a school, and even the development of painting advance toward works in which a whole series of achievements are resumed, that is, toward *masterpieces* in which what was sought until then is finally achieved and which, at least for a while, render useless the earlier attempts, or in any case are permanent landmarks in the progress of painting. . . .

In short, the relation between the painter and his model, as expressed in classical painting, also presupposes a certain idea of the communication between the painter and the viewer of his paintings. When the classical painter in front of his canvas looks for an expression of objects and beings that will preserve all their richness and lose none of their properties, it is because he wants to be as convincing as the things themselves. It is because he believes he can reach us only the way they reach us, namely, by imposing upon *our senses* an unimpeachable spectacle. All of classical painting rests on this idea of a communication between the painter and his public through the evidence of things. The modern problem of knowing how the painter's intention will be reborn in those who look at his paintings is not even raised by classical painting, which, in order to achieve communication, relies upon the perceptual apparatus considered as a *natural* means of communication between men. Do we not all have eyes which function much the same way? If the painter has known how to discover sufficient signs of depth or of velvet, will we not all, when we look at the picture, see the same spectacle, endowed with the same sort of evidence that belongs to perceived things?

However, even if classical painting set itself the goal of representing nature and human nature, it is still true that its painters were painters, and no worthwhile painting has ever consisted in simple representation. Malraux often points out that the modern conception of painting as *creative* expression was a novelty for the public much more than for the painters themselves, who have always practiced it, even if unconsciously and without formulating it theoretically. Painters have for this reason often anticipated what we practice, so that they remain the appointed mediators in any initiation to painting. We would then have to believe that, with their eyes fixed upon the world and at the very moment when they believed they were asking it for the secret of a sufficient representation, they unwittingly brought about that transformation or metamorphosis which painting later made its express purpose. But to define classical painting it is surely not enough to speak about *representation* or *nature*, or refer to *our senses* as natural means of communication. That is not how classical painting reaches us. It is not even how classical painting reached its first viewers. We must find a way of uniting its elements of creation and its element of representation.

Perhaps we can manage this by examining more closely one of the means of "representation" of which classical painting was most often proud, namely, perspective, and by showing that in reality it was created from nothing. Malraux sometimes speaks as if the *senses* and sense-data had never varied throughout the centuries and as if the classical perspective was imperative so long as it referred to them. Yet it is certain that classical perspective is not a law of perceptual behavior. It derives from the cultural order, as one of the ways man has invented for projecting before himself the perceived world, and is not a copy of this world. If we compare the rules of perspective with the world of spontaneous vision, it is immediately clear that they form an optional interpretation, although perhaps more probable than others—not because the perceived world contradicts the laws of perspective and imposes others but rather because it does not demand any one in particular and belongs to another order than these rules. We should not tire of referring to the fine observations of the psychologists who have shown that, in free and spontaneous perception, objects spread out in depth do not have any definite apparent size. Distant objects are not even bigger than perspective leads us to believe. The moon on the horizon is not "bigger" than the coin I hold—at least not the size that is supposed to be common to these two objects. The moon is a "large object in the distance." The size in question is, like hot or cold, a quality which adheres to the moon and cannot be measured by a certain number of *partes aliquoties* of the coin.

The near object and the far object are not comparable. All we can say is that one is near and absolutely "tiny" and the other far and absolutely "big." If I want to pass from this to perspective, I must cease to look freely over the whole spectacle, close one eye, and circumscribe my vision. I must take the object in my hand as the reference point for what I call the apparent size of the moon and of the coin and then transfer the common measures I obtain into the single dimension of the paper. But during this time the perceived world has disappeared. I cannot obtain the common denominator or the common measure which allows projection in a single plane except by renouncing the simultaneity of objects. While I was seeing the coin and the moon in one view, my look had to be fixed on one of them, so that the other one appeared to be on the margin—a little-object-seen-close, or a big-object-seen-far-off—incommensurable with the first and as though situated in another universe. What I transfer on the paper is not this coexistence of the perceived objects and their rivalry within my vision. I find the means of arbitrating their conflict, and this is what makes depth. I decide to make them cohabit in the same plane. I succeed in this by substituting for the total spectacle and by coagulating on paper a series of local and monocular views, of which none is superimposable upon the parts of the living perceptual field.

In spontaneous vision, things rivaled one another for my look and, being anchored in one of them, I felt the solicitation of the others which made them coexist with the first. Thus at every moment I was swimming in the world of things and overrun by a horizon of things to see which could not possibly be seen simultaneously with what I was seeing but *by this very fact* were simultaneous with it. But in perspective I construct a representation in which each thing ceases to demand the whole visual field for itself, makes concessions to the others, and agrees to occupy no more space on the paper than the others leave it. In the first case, my glance, running freely over depth, height, and width, was not subordinated to any point of view, because it adopted and rejected each one in turn. In perspective, I renounce that ambiguity and agree to let only that figure in my drawing which could be seen from a certain reference point by an immobile eye fixed on a certain "vanishing point" of a certain "vanishing line," chosen once and for all. In spontaneous vision, I had the experience of a world of teeming, exclusive things which could be embraced only by means of a temporal cycle in which each gain is simultaneously a loss. In the other case, this world crystallizes into an ordered perspective within which backgrounds resign themselves to being merely backgrounds, inaccessible and vague as required, where objects in the foreground lose something of their aggressiveness, order their interior lines according to the common law of the spectacle, already preparing to become backgrounds when necessary, and where finally nothing looks into one's vision and adopts the figure of being present. The whole scene is in the past, in the mode of completion and eternity. Everything adopts an air of propriety and discretion. Things no longer call upon me and I am not compromised by them.

If we add to the artifice of geometric perspective that of aerial perspective, as, for example, in so many Venetian paintings, we can feel how far the painter of a landscape and the spectator before a painting are above the world, how they dominate it, how they embrace it with their look. Perspective is much more than a secret technique for imitating a reality given as such to all men. It is the very realization and invention of a world dominated and possessed through and through in an instantaneous system, which spontaneous vision at best sketches, trying vainly to hold together all the things which clamor for its whole attention. Geometrical perspective is no more the only way of looking at the sensible world than the classical portrait is the only view of man. These faces, always subordinated to a character, a passion, or a mood—always signifying—presuppose the same relation between man and the world as can be seen in a classical landscape, the relation of the adult sure of himself to the world he dominates. The expression of childhood in classical painting is never that of childhood in its own lived terms. It is the pensive look that we sometimes admire in babies or animals because we take it as a sign of adult meditation, whereas it is only ignorance of our world. Before being, and in order to be, the representation of a reality or the study of an object, classical painting should first be the metamorphosis of the perceived world into a precise and rational universe, and the transformation of empirical man, with his confusion and uncertainty, into an identifiable character.

It is important to understand that classical painting is a creation, and that it is creative in the very moment when it seeks to be the representation of a reality. Thus what we make of modern painting depends upon how we regard classical painting. As long as we believe that the objectivity of the classics is justified by the natural functioning of our senses and grounded in the evidence of perception, any other alternative can consist only in breaking with objectivity and perception and turning toward the individual, making painting a ceremony in his honor. Henceforth there is only one subject in painting, namely, the painter himself.[1] There is no longer a search for the velvet of peaches, as in Chardin, but, as in Braque, for the velvet of the painting. Whereas the classical painters were themselves unwittingly, modern painters want first of all to be original, and their power of expression becomes confused with their individual difference.[2] Since painting is no longer for faith or for beauty, it is for the individual;[3] it is the annexation of the world by the individual.[4] Thus the artist joins "the household of the ambitious and the addicted,"[5] devoted like them to a single stubborn and monotonous pleasure, a self-pleasure which is the most individual pleasure, the least cultivated pleasure, a demonic pleasure in everything that in man destroys man. . . .

1. André Malraux, *Le Musée imaginaire, la psychologie de l'art* (Paris: Skira, 1947), p. 59. [EDITOR: All the citations from Malraux are taken from this edition; it was not possible to refer to the Gallimard edition of *The Voices of Silence*, since the two texts published by the author are quite different. TRANSLATOR: The precise reference is to the three-volume *Essais de psychologie de l'art* (Paris: Skira, 1947–50), of which the first is *Le Musée imaginaire* (1947); the second, *La Création artistique* (1948); and the third, *La Monnaie de l'absolu* (1950).]

2. *Ibid.*, p. 79.

3. *Ibid.*, p. 83.

4. Malraux, *La Monnaie de l'absolu*, p. 118.

5. Malraux, *La Création artistique*, p. 144.

But Malraux is well aware that there is more than that to modern painting and that it would be difficult to apply this definition to Cézanne or Klee, for example. To be sure, some painters present sketches as paintings which classical painters would have kept for themselves, even when they were more eloquent than their paintings, or would have tried to translate into the quite explicit language of a finished work. Clearly, for certain modern painters, the canvas is nothing but the signature, the trace of a moment of life. It must be seen in an exposition of a series of successive works, whereas the classical canvas was sufficient to itself and offered itself for contemplation. But the tolerance of the incomplete may mean two things. It may be that the moderns have in fact renounced the masterpiece and no longer seek anything but the immediate expression of the moment, of feeling, and of the individual—of the "brute expression," as Malraux says. Or it may mean that completion, the presentation that is objective and convincing for the senses, may no longer be considered necessary or even sufficient and thus that the proper sign of the complete work has been found elsewhere. Baudelaire wrote, in a line that Malraux recalls, "that a complete work was not necessarily finished and a finished work not necessarily complete."[6] Let us emphasize the last words. Then we shall understand that the moderns, at any rate the better and more worthwhile ones, do not seek the incomplete for its own sake but value more than the moment when the work is *finished* only that moment, precocious or late, when the spectator is reached by the canvas and mysteriously resumes in his own way the meaning of the gesture through which it was made. Skipping the intermediaries, without any other guide than a certain movement discovered in the line or an almost immaterial trace of the brush, the spectator then rejoins the silent world of the painter, henceforth uttered and accessible.

There exists the improvisation of child prodigies who have not learned their own gesture. They allow themselves to be possessed and dissolved by the moment and, on the pretext that a painter is a hand, think it is enough to have a hand with which to paint.

6. Malraux, *Le Musée imaginaire*, p. 63.

They extract small wonders from their bodies, as a morose young man who observes his body with sufficient complacency can always find some little peculiarity in it to feed his self-worship or his religion of psychoanalysis. But there is also the improvisation of the artist who has turned toward the world, whose work is a bridge to the other, and who has finally composed for himself an expressive organ, like an acquired voice which is more his own than any of its first efforts. There is the improvisation of automatic writing and there is that of *The Charterhouse of Parma.* One of the grandeurs of modern thought and modern art is to have loosened the false lines which tied a valuable work to the finished work. Since perception itself is never *finished,* since it gives us a world to express and think only through these partial perspectives which it envelops and whose ineffable evidence is not the kind we possess, and since, finally, this world announces itself only through lightning signs as a spoken word, the permission not to "finish" is not necessarily a preference accorded the individual over the world, to the nonsignifying over the signifying. It may also be the recognition of a mode of communication which does not pass through objective evidence, a signification which does not refer to an already given object but constitutes and inaugurates its object—as such it would not be prosaic, because it awakens and rallies our whole power of expression and comprehension. Modern painting poses a quite different problem from that of the individual, namely, the question of knowing how one can communicate without the aid of a preestablished nature upon which all men's senses open and of knowing how there can be communication prior to communication and, finally, how there can be a reason before reason.

On this point Malraux in certain parts of his book surpasses his questionable theses on the individualism of modern painting. Then he goes further than anyone else since Husserl introduced the notion of *style* to translate our original relation to the world. What the painter tries to put into his painting is not his immediate self, the very nuance of feeling, but his style. He must master his style as much in his own attempts, in his own person, as in others' paintings or in the world. What a long time it takes, says Malraux, before a writer learns to speak with his own voice.

Similarly, what a long time it takes the painter who does not, like the historian of art, have his work spread out before him but *creates* it and must pick out the features discernible in his early canvases that will become his finished work, provided he does not mistake himself. . . . Actually, he does not discern himself even in these canvases. The painter is no more capable of seeing his paintings than the writer is able to read his own work. These painted canvases and these books have a much too immediate resemblance to the horizon and the ground of their life for one or the other to experience the phenomenon of expression with all its contrast. There must be other internal movements for the power of these works to burst forth and thus awaken the significations of which they were incapable. Indeed, it is only through these movements that the significations are significations. For the writer or for the painter, there is only one's allusion to oneself in the familiarity of one's personal vibration, pompously called an internal monologue, and no less deceiving than that we hold with our body, or, as Malraux rightly says in *The Human Condition,* than our voice "heard by the throat." The painter leaves his wake but, except when he amuses himself with earlier works by discovering what he has become, he does not very much like to look at it. He prefers to have it behind him. For him, everything still lies in the present, and the feeble accent of his early works is eminently contained in the language of his maturity, just as Euclidean geometry is a special case of some general geometry. Without looking back on their earlier works and by the sole fact that they have fulfilled certain expressive operations, the writer and the painter are endowed with new organs, as it were. In this new condition, they experience the excess of what is *to be said* beyond their ordinary capacities—unless a mysterious fatigue, of which there are historical examples, intervenes. They are able to pursue the same meaning "further," as though they fed on their own substance and grew from their own gifts, as if every step taken made the next one possible, or finally, as if each successful expression prescribed another task for the spiritual automaton or founded an institution whose efficacy it could never establish once and for all.

Thus this "inner schema" which becomes more and more imperious with each task—to the point that the famous chair becomes *for us* "a brutal ideogram of the very name Van Gogh" [7] —is legible *for Van Gogh* neither in his early works nor even in what is called his interior life. If it were, Van Gogh would not have needed painting to find himself and would have stopped painting. He is this life insofar as it emerges from its inherence and its silence, insofar as its essential difference ceases to indulge itself and becomes a means of understanding and making understood, of seeing and of offering something to be seen—and thus not shut up in some private laboratory, in the depths of the mute individual, but diffused through its commerce with the visible world, spread out in everything it sees. Style is what makes all signification possible. Before signs or emblems become for everyone, even the artist, the simple index of already given significations, there must be that fruitful moment when signs have *given form* to experience or when an operant and latent meaning finds the emblems which should liberate it, making it manageable for the artist and accessible to others. If we really want to understand the origin of signification—and, unless we do, we shall not understand any other creation or any other culture, for we shall fall back upon the supposition of an intelligible world in which everything is signified in advance—we must give up every signification that is already institutionalized and return to the starting point of a nonsignifying world. This is always what faces the creator, at least with respect to what he is about to say. Let us not underestimate the problem. It is not a question of understanding how signification, ideas, or given propositions are to be applied to this object or what unforeseeable shape knowledge will assume in this circumstance. We must first of all understand how this object or this circumstance begins to signify itself and under what conditions. To the extent that the painter has already painted and is in some measure master of himself, what is given to him with his style is not a certain number of ideas or tics that he can inventory but a manner of formulation that is just as recognizable for others and just as little visible to him as his silhouette or his everyday gestures.

7. *Ibid.*, pp. 79–80.

Thus, when Malraux writes that style is the "means of re-creating the world according to the values of the man who discovers it," [8] or that it is the "expression of a meaning lent to the world, a call for and not a consequence of a way of seeing," [9] or finally that it is "the reduction to a fragile human perspective of the eternal world which draws us along according to a mysterious rhythm into a drift of stars," [10] his definitions do not get to the heart of the phenomenon. They are not at the point where style is at work. They are retrospective, pointing to some of style's consequences but not what is essential. When style is at work, the painter knows nothing of the antithesis of man and the world, of signification and the absurd, since man and signification are sketching themselves against the background of the world through the very operation of style. If this notion deserves, as we believe, the credit given it by Malraux, it is on the condition that it be primary. Style therefore cannot be taken as an object, since it is still nothing and will become visible only in the work. We cannot even say with certainty that style is a means of representation, because that would presuppose some exterior model for it and assume a finished painting before it is painted. But neither can we say that the representation of the world is "a *stylistic means*," [11] which would make it known in advance like an *end*. We must see it emerging at the point of contact between the painter and the world, in the hollow of the painter's perception, and as an exigency which arises from that perception.

Malraux demonstrates this in one of his better passages: perception already stylizes. A woman passing by is not first and foremost a corporeal contour for me, a colored mannequin, a spectacle in a given spot. She is "an individual, sentimental, sexual expression." She is a flesh in its full presence, with its vigor and weakness there in her walk or the click of her heel on the ground. She is a unique way of varying the accent of feminine being and thus of human being, which I understand the way I understand

8. Malraux, *La Création artistique*, p. 151.
9. *Ibid.*, p. 154.
10. *Ibid.*
11. As Malraux says in *ibid.*, p. 158.

a sentence, namely, because it finds in me the system of resonators that it needs. Thus perception already stylizes, that is, it affects all the elements of a body or behavior with a certain common deviation with respect to some familiar norm that I have behind me. But if I am not a painter, the woman passing by speaks only to my body or to my sense of life. If I am a painter, this first signification will arouse another. I am going to do more than select from my usual perception and translate lines, colors, traces on to the canvas, and these only so that *among* them there appears the vital or sensual value of the woman. My choice and the gestures which guide it will also be ruled by a more restrictive condition. Everything I found, compared to the actual "observable," will be subject to a more secret principle of distortion which ultimately works so that what the viewer sees on the canvas is not merely the evocation of a woman, of a trade, or of a pose, or even a "concept of life" (that of the model or the painter), but another typical way of inhabiting the world, of handling it, and of interpreting it through a face as much as by dress, as much through the flesh as through the spirit.

"All style is giving form to the elements of the world which permits the orientation of the world to one of its essential parts." [12] Signification occurs where we subject the given elements of the world to a "coherent deformation." [13] But how does it happen that the world appears coherent to us and that all the visible and moral vectors in a painting converge toward the same signification X? They cannot, as we have already said, refer to any preestablished order of significations. Therefore the world perceived by man must be such that, through a certain arrangement of elements, we are able to make appear in it emblems not only of our instinctive intentions but even of our most intimate relation to being. The perceived world and perhaps even the world of thought are so made that whatever we place in them immediately acquires a meaning in terms of a language of which we become the speakers but which is a task as much as a legacy. It is suffi-

12. Cited by Maurice Blanchot, "Le Musée, l'art et le temps," *Critique*, no. 43 (December, 1950), p. 204.

13. Malraux, *La Création artistique*, p. 152.

cient that we shape in the manifold of things certain hollows, certain fissures—and we do this the moment we are alive—to bring into the world that which is strangest to it: *a meaning*, an incitement, sister to those who draw us into the present or the future, toward being or nonbeing. . . . Style exists (and hence signification) as soon as there are figures and backgrounds, a norm and a deviation, a top and a bottom, that is, as soon as certain elements of the world assume the value of dimensions to which subsequently all the rest relate and through which we can point them out. For each painter, style is the system of equivalences he builds for himself for this work of manifestation. It is the general and concrete index of the "coherent deformation" through which he focuses the signification still scattered in his perception and gives it an express existence.

Pictorial expression assumes and transcends the patterning of the world which begins in perception. In other words, the work is not fashioned far from things and in some intimate laboratory to which the painter alone possesses a key. This also means that from its side the work is not an arbitrary decree and that it always relates to *its* world as if the principle of equivalences through which it manifests the world had always been buried in it. Writers should not underestimate the painter's *labor* and *study* and, on the pretext that basically painting is painting and not speech, forget what is methodical in the painter's research. It is true that, scarcely having drawn his system of equivalences from the world, the painter invests it again in colors and a space on a canvas; meaning impregnates the canvas more than the canvas expresses meaning. "That yellow rent on the sky over Golgotha . . . is a thing made from anguish, an anguish which has turned into a yellow rent in the sky and which is immediately submerged and thickened by the qualities appropriate to things." [14] More than being manifested by the painting, the meaning sinks into it and trembles around it "like a wave of heat." [15] It is "like an immense and futile effort, always arrested halfway

14. Jean-Paul Sartre, *Situations II* (Paris: Gallimard, 1948), p. 61.

15. *Ibid.*, p. 60.

between heaven and earth," [16] to express what the nature of painting prevents it from expressing. For professional users of language, such an impression is perhaps inevitable. The same thing happens to them that happens to us when we hear a foreign language that we speak poorly. We find it monotonous and marked with a heavy unvaried flavor, precisely because we have not made it the principal instrument of our relations with the world. The meaning of the painting is lost for those of us for whom painting is not the way of communicating with the world. But for the painter—and even for all the enthusiasts of painting—the meaning is more than a wave of heat at the surface of the canvas, since it is capable of demanding *that* color or *that* object in preference to all others, and since it commands the arrangement of a painting just as imperiously as a syntax or a logic. . . . To be sure, the meaning of that yellow rent in the sky over Golgotha remains captive of the color, as the fleecy remains captive of blue, or the acid gaiety of the green apple. But the whole of the painting does not lie there. That anguish adhering to the color is only a component in total meaning that is less pathetic, more durable, more *readable,* and it will remain in us long after our eyes have left the painting.

Malraux is quite right to relate the anecdote of the innkeeper at Cassis who, seeing Renoir at work by the sea, approaches him: "There were some nude women bathing in some other place. Goodness knows what he was looking at, and he changed only a little corner." Malraux continues: "The blue of the sea had become that of the brook in *The Bathers*. . . . This vision was less a way of looking at the sea than the secret elaboration of a world to which that depth of blue whose immensity he was recapturing pertained." [17] But why, exactly, did the blue of the sea belong to the world of Renoir's painting? Because each fragment of the world, and in particular of the sea, sometimes riddled with eddies and ripples and plumed with spray, sometimes massive, murky, and immobile in itself, assumes limitless shapes of being.

16. *Ibid.*, p. 61.
17. Malraux, *La Création artistique,* p. 113.

And, in the special way each fragment has of responding and vibrating to the encounter with one's glance, it evokes all sorts of variations and thus teaches, beyond itself, a general way of speaking. It is possible to paint nude women and a fresh-water brook by the sea at Cassis, because all that is asked of the sea is its way of interpreting the liquid substance, of exhibiting it and composing it with itself to make it say this and that, in sum, to make it a type of all the appearances of water. It is possible to paint while looking at the world, because the style which will define the painter for others appears to him to be found in the appearances themselves (insofar, of course, as they are appearances that he has).

If Western painting, as Malraux remarks, has varied its subjects so little, if, for example, from generation to generation, from Rembrandt to Soutine, the flayed ox reappears, that is because it is not necessary patiently to explore everything in order to reach painting. It is not even a bad thing, in order to manifest a style, to treat again a subject with which one has already dealt. For painting is a system of equivalences and significations which it is more convincing to take to the level of a familiar or frequently painted object than to an unknown object where the equivalences and significations risk being engulfed. "A certain peremptory equilibrium or disequilibrium of colors and lines overwhelms the person who discovers that the half-opened door over there is that of another world." [18] "Another world"—by this we mean the same world that the painter sees and that speaks his own language, but freed from the nameless weight which held it back and kept it equivocal. How could the painter or the poet be anything else than his encounter with this world? Austerity and the obsession with surfaces or geometrical forms still have an odor of life, even if it is a shameful or despairing life. The painter rearranges the prosaic world and, so to speak, makes a holocaust of objects, just as poetry melts ordinary language. But in the case of works that one likes to see or read again, the disorder is always another order. It is a new system of equivalences which

18. *Ibid.*, p. 142.

demands *this* upheaval and not just any one, and it is in the name of a *truer* relation among things that their ordinary ties are broken.

A poet has received, once and for all, the task of translating these words, this voice, this accent whose echo is returned to him by each thing and each circumstance. There are no changes in ordinary language that he rejects in order to get on with his job, and he does not propose any that are not motivated. In his first draft of *The Idiot*, Dostoevski made Myshkin the assassin. In the next, it was Rogozhin. But the substitution is not without significance. It is founded on the system of equivalences or, rather, on the principle of selection and the rule of expression prescribed by this novel, destined as it was to communicate this rather than that. "The character is replaced by another, just as in a painting a window that is too light for the wall in which it is set is replaced by iron rails." [19] The ordinary meaning of the window, the iron railings, the wall is not negated, since one is always talking about the world if one wants to be understood. It is at least reintegrated into a more originary and longer meaning from which it is taken. The look of the wall, the window, the pipes no longer serves only to indicate, beyond itself, things to be used. Rather—since perception is always action—here the action becomes praxis, that is, it rejects the abstractions of the useful and refuses to sacrifice the means to the end or appearance to reality. Henceforth everything has a value, and the uses of objects count less than their capacity for composing all together, even in their intimate texture, a valid emblem of the world with which we are confronted.

It is not surprising that this unblinkered vision and unbiased action should throw words out of focus and regroup them and the objects of the world. But nothing would be more foolish than to imagine it would be enough to smash language in order to write *Les Illuminations*. Malraux remarks profoundly of modern painters that, "although no one of them spoke of truth, all, faced with the works of their adversaries, spoke of imposture." [20] They

19. *Ibid.*, p. 147.
20. Malraux, *La Monnaie de l'absolu*, p. 125.

want nothing to do with a truth defined as the resemblance of painting and the world. They would accept the idea of a truth defined as a painting's cohesion with itself, as the presence of a unique principle in it which affects each means of expression with a certain contextual value. The classical painters, whose art went beyond that, at least lived in the comfortable illusion of a technique of painting that would enable them to get at velvet itself or space itself. . . . The moderns know very well that there is no spectacle in the world—far less a painting—which absolutely imposes itself upon perception, whereas the imperious stroke of the brush can do more to make our look possess the wool or the flesh than the most patient reconstruction of appearances. But the moderns have not put chaos in the place of the mind's inspection of the very texture of things—they have introduced the allusive logic of world.

Modern painters mean to signify no less than the classics and they retain the idea of something to say which one can more or less approximate. It is simply that Van Gogh's "going further" at the moment he paints *The Crows* no longer indicates some reality toward which one must go. It shows what still must be done in order to restore the encounter between his glance and the things which solicit it, between the body and the world it inhabits—the encounter between the one who has to exist with what does exist. If it is this encounter which art signifies, it is very clear that art cannot achieve it by *resembling* things or the world. "As always in art, one must lie to tell the truth," Sartre rightly says. It is said that the exact recording of a conversation which had seemed brilliant later gives the impression of indigence. The truth lies here. The conversation reproduced exactly is no longer what it was while we were living it. It lacks the presence of those who were speaking, the whole surplus of meaning yielded by the gestures and faces that especially give the impression of something happening, of a discovery and continuous innovation. The conversation no longer exists. It does not ramify in all directions—it *is*, flattened out in the single dimension of sound. Instead of summoning our whole being, it does no more than touch us lightly by ear. That is, in order to satisfy us as it does, the work of art—which also usually addresses only one of our senses and in any case never has the kind of presence that belongs to lived experience—must have the capacity for more than a frozen existence. It must have the capacity for a sublimated existence, one more true than truth itself. Modern painting, like modern thought generally, absolutely obliges us to admit a truth which does not resemble things, which is without any external model and without any predestined instruments of expression, and which is nevertheless truth.

But it may be objected that, if painting is really a language, there should be a way of putting into articulated language what painting expresses in its way. What does it say?

If we put the painter back in contact with his world, as we are trying to do, perhaps we shall find less enigmatic that metamorphosis which through him transforms the world into painting, or that which changes the painter from his beginnings to his maturing into himself, or, finally, the metamorphosis which in each generation revives certain works of the past and obtains an echo from them which they had never previously given. When a writer considers painters, he is a little in the position of readers in relation to the writer. "What? is this what the writer I admire so much does with his time? Is that the house he lives in? Is that the woman with whom he shares his life? Are these the petty problems that obsess him?" We think of the writer in terms of his work—the way we think of an absent woman in terms of the circumstances, words, and attitudes in which she expressed herself most purely. When we meet again the woman we love, or make the writer's acquaintance, we feel foolishly disappointed at not finding, in each moment of the person's presence, that brilliant essence, that impeccable speech that we become accustomed to associating with that person's name. But that is only prestige (sometimes even envy, secret hatred). The next stage of maturity is to understand that there are no supermen, that there is no man who does not have a man's life to live. The secret of the woman loved, of the writer, or of the painter does not lie in some realm beyond his empirical life. It is so mixed in with his mediocre experiences, so modestly confused with his perception of the world, that there can be no question of his meeting it face to face apart from his life.

While reading Malraux's *Psychology of Art*, we sometimes receive the impression that he, who certainly knows all this as a writer, forgets it where painters are concerned and dedicates the same kind of cult to them which we believe he would not accept from his readers—he transforms painters into gods. "What genius is not fascinated by that extremity of painting, by that appeal before which time itself vacillates? It is the moment of possession of the world. Let painting go no further, and Hals the Elder becomes God." [21] Perhaps this is the painter seen by others. For himself, he is nothing of the kind. He is a man at work who each morning finds in the shape of things the same questioning and the same call to which he never stops responding. His work is never completed; it is always in progress. One day, life reveals itself; the body is written off. At other times—and more sadly—the question scattered through the spectacles of the world ceases to be heard. Then he is not a painter any more, or he is an honorary painter. But as long as he paints, his painting is always open onto things. If he is or becomes blind, his painting is open to that unimpeachable individual which gave itself to him, from the first day of his life, as that which had to be made manifest. And that is why the painter's labor, which is obscure for him, is nevertheless guided and oriented. He himself sees only the outline, and it is only the others who can see where he is, because what is implicitly given to him at each minute of his experience cannot in his eyes have the relief and expected contour that it has in the life of another person. But this blind passage is nevertheless staked out with signs; it never creates in the void, *ex nihilo*. It is always only a question of advancing the line of the already opened furrow and of recapturing and generalizing an accent which has already appeared in the corner of a previous painting or in some moment of his experience. The painter himself can never say—since the distinction has no meaning—what comes from him and what comes from things,

21. Malraux, *La Création artistique*, p. 150.

what the new work adds to the old ones, what he has taken from this, and what is his own.

There is a triple resumption through which he continues while going beyond, conserves while destroying, interprets through deviation, and infuses a new meaning into what nevertheless called for and anticipated it. It is not simply a metamorphosis in the fairy tale sense of a miracle or magic, violence, or aggression. It is not an absolute creation in an absolute solitude. It is also a response to what the world, the past, and previous works demanded of him, namely, accomplishment and fraternity. Husserl has used the fine word *Stiftung*—foundation, institution—to designate, first, the unlimited fecundity of each present which, precisely because it is singular and passes, can never stop having been and thus being universally. Above all, he has used *Stiftung* to designate that fecundity of the products of culture which continue to have a value after their historical appearance and open a field of work beyond and the same as their own. It is thus that the world as soon as he has seen it, his first attempts at painting, and the whole past of painting create for the painter a *tradition, that is,* Husserl says, *the power to forget origins,* the duty to start over again and to give the past, not survival, which is the hypocritical form of forgetfulness, but the efficacy of renewal or "repetition," which is the noble form of memory.

Malraux emphasizes the deceptive and derisory in the comedy of the mind; those contemporary rivals, Delacroix and Ingres, whom prosterity regards as twins. Those painters who want to be classic and, on the contrary, are only neoclassic. Or those styles which escape their creator's view and become visible only when the museum gathers together works scattered around the world or when photography enlarges miniatures, transforms a section of a painting by its way of framing it, changes rugs, coins, and stained-glass windows into paintings, and brings to painting a consciousness of itself which is always retrospective.

> As if an imaginary spirit of art pushed forward from miniature to painting and from fresco to stained-glass window in a single conquest which it suddenly abandoned for another, parallel or suddenly opposed, as if a subterranean torment of history unified all

> these scattered works by dragging them along with it [. . .]. A style known in its evolution and metamorphoses becomes less an idea than the illusion of a living fatality. Reproduction, and reproduction alone, has brought into art those imaginary superartists who have a clouded birth, a life with its conquests and concessions to the taste for wealth or seduction, a death agony, and a resurrection—and are called styles.[22]

But if expression is creative with regard to what it transforms,* and *precisely because expression always goes beyond what it transforms* by bringing it into a composition which changes its meaning, the same was already true of times preceding ours and even of our perception of the world before painting, since that perception already marked things with the trace of human elaboration. Our expressive arts transcend their starting points toward another art. But these data themselves transcend previous acts of expression toward a future that is ourselves, and in this sense they call for the very metamorphosis we impose on them. One can no more inventory a painting—say what is there and what is not—than one can inventory a vocabulary, and for the same reason. Neither is a sum of signs but a new organ of human culture which does not open up a finite number of movements but rather a general type of conduct and a field of investigations.

22. Malraux, *Le Musée imaginaire,* p. 52.

* 1) The transformation (in this case, or in general that of the past by the present, of the world by painting, or of the painter's past by his present) is nevertheless not a masquerade. It is possible only because the datum *was painting,* because there is a logos of the sensible world (and of the social world and human history)—Malraux's analytic illusion and the phenomenon of the *cultural world.* There is the only mystery: that of the *Nachvollzug.* It rests on the mystery of the natural world and its logos. Man transcends the natural world inadvertently and naturally, as it were—historicity "a subterranean torrent" and the internal historicity between man and man, between man and the world. Profane or prosaic and sacred historicity. 2) Everything, then, that is true of painting is also true of language (Descartes, Stendhal, our unity with them). Against the idea of an *action* of language which [would be?] really ours. 3) What remains to be done (the last question to be put to logic): the sedimentation of art collapses to the extent that it is achieved. With that exception, we should really suspend "signifying" language to allow "pure" language to appear, for language is painting as painting is language. We must get rid of the illusion of possession through saying.

It is as Malraux has said: the metamorphosis through which we discover the classical painters, who were convinced of exploring a reality, and painting, in the modern sense, is not fortuitous. The classics were also already painters in the modern sense. When atheistic thought revives works which believed themselves to be in the service of the holy or absolute without being able to share the religious experience to which they belonged, there is no masquerade involved. It gives them back to themselves and confronts them with the interrogation from which they were born. We are able to find something in forms of art which historically belong to very different experiences than our own because after all they have something to say to us and because their artists, believing that they were continuing primitive terrors or those of Asia and Egypt, secretly inaugurated another history, which is still ours and makes them present to us, while the empires and beliefs to which they thought they *belonged* have long ago disappeared. If a map by Georges de La Tour, or a fragment of a painting by ———, makes us think of nineteenth-century painting, the reason certainly is not that La Tour was ——— or Manet, although La Tour and ——— were painters in the same sense as Manet—the reason is that they belonged to the same universe.[23]

Malraux shows perfectly that what makes "a Vermeer" for us is not that this canvas was painted one day by the hand of the man Vermeer. It is the fact that it embodies the "Vermeer structure" or that it speaks the language of Vermeer, that is, it observes the system of equivalences according to which each one of its elements, like a hundred pointers on a hundred dials, marks the same deviation. If this same Vermeer, when very old, had painted a picture from bits and pieces without any coherence, it would not have been a "real Vermeer." By contrast, if a counterfeiter succeeded in capturing not only the writing but even the style of the great Vermeers, he would no longer be quite a counterfeiter. He would be one of those painters who worked in the studio of the classical painters and painted for them.* In-

23. EDITOR: The blanks are in the text.
* Quasi platonism.

deed, such counterfeiting is impossible. To be able to repeat the style of Vermeer after centuries of other painting and once the meaning of the problem of painting itself has changed, the counterfeiter would have to be a painter himself—in which case he would not do "fake Vermeers." He would be making, between two original paintings, a study "after Vermeer" or a "tribute to Vermeer" in which he would invest himself.

What betrays the counterfeiter and makes him one is not that his paintings resemble those of Vermeer but that they do not resemble them enough. The history of painting cannot always tell whether or not a painting is from the hand of the individual Vermeer who inhabited a perishable body. That is not how we distinguish the real Vermeer from the fake, *that is not even what distinguishes them as to their truth.* Because he was a great painter, Vermeer has become something of an institution or an entity. Just as history must discover the meaning of parliament under the Old Regime or the meaning of the French Revolution, and to do so must put things in perspective, treating this as essential and that as an accidental feature of parliament or the Revolution, so the history of painting must define, from among the actual canvases attributed to Vermeer, an essence, a structure, a style, a meaning of Vermeer against which the discordant elements, if there are any, that fatigue, circumstance, or custom has torn from his brush cannot prevail. We should not say just that, without evidence, the historians of painting can judge authenticity only through examining the painting itself. This is not an imperfection in our knowledge and history. It is the very nature of history when it comes to its task of comprehending the facts. Even in law, a complete catalogue of the master's works is not indispensable and does not suffice to establish what is really *by him.* For before history his work is nothing more than a certain word spoken in the dialogue of painting. And what he may have said by chance does not enter the record, as though one should attribute to him, if such a thing were possible, what others have said exactly as if he had said it. Not against but quite beyond empirical history, which attends only to empirical events and is blind to their contents, another history is being written which distinguishes what events confuse and also brings together what they separated, describing the rise of styles, their mutations, their surprising transformations, and also and simultaneously their solidarity in a single history of painting.

The first sketches on the walls of caves opened a limitless field of discovery. They set forth the world "to be painted" or "to be sketched," calling for an indefinite future of painting, so that they speak to us and we answer them by metamorphoses in which they collaborate with us. There are two historicities. One is chronic or even derisory, full of misunderstandings, in which each age struggles against the others as against aliens by composing its concerns and perspectives upon them. This historicity is forgetfulness rather than memory. It is dismemberment, ignorance, externality. But the other historicity, without which the first would be impossible, is the *interest* which attaches us to what is not ourselves. It is the life which the past in a continuous exchange finds in us and brings to us. It is, above all, the life which this historicity continues to lead in each artist who revives, renews, and recaptures with each painting the entire undertaking of the past.

In this respect the Museum's function, like the library's, is not entirely beneficent. It certainly enables us to see works that were scattered around the world and engulfed in the cults or civilizations which they sought to ornament as unified aspects of a single effort. In this sense our consciousness of painting as painting is based upon the Museum. But painting is to be found in each painter at work, and there it is in a pure state, whereas the Museum associates it with lesser qualities. One should go to the Museum the way painters go there, in the joy of dialogue, and not as we amateurs go, with our spurious reverence. The Museum gives us a false consciousness, a thief's conscience. We occasionally sense that these works were not intended to *end up* between these bare walls for the pleasure of Sunday strollers, for children on their free afternoon from school, or for Monday intellectuals. We sense vaguely that something has been lost and that these gatherings of old maids, this silence of the grave, and the respect of pygmies do not constitute the true milieu of art. So much effort, so many joys and sorrows, so much anger and labor were not destined to reflect one day the sad light of the Louvre museum. . . .

The Museum transforms efforts into works. It allows only styles to appear but also adds a false prestige to their true value by detaching them from the chance circumstances in which they arose and making us believe that some superartists or "fatalities" guided the artists' hands from the very beginning. Whereas the style of each painter throbbed in him like his deepest heartbeat and, insofar as he is speech and style, resonated in all other artists' speech and style, experiencing the kindred value of their efforts,[24] the Museum converts this secret, modest, nondeliberate, and almost involuntary historicity into an official and pompous history. The unsuspected imminence of a regression gives our enjoyment of a given painter a pathetic nuance which was quite foreign to him. He himself labored happily his whole life, a man unaware that he was on a volcano, while we see his work as flowers on the edge of a precipice. The Museum makes painters as mysterious for us as octapuses or lobsters. It transforms these works, created in the heat of life, into marvels from another world. In the pensive light of the Museum and under its glass panes, the breath which sustained these works becomes no more than a feeble palpitation on their surface. . . . The Museum kills the vehemence of painting just as the library, as Sartre says, transforms writings which were once a man's gestures into *messages*. It is the historicity of death. But there is a living historicity of which the Museum offers only a broken image. It is the historicity that dwells in the painter at work when, in a single gesture, he binds the tradition he continues into the tradition he founds. It is the historicity which in a single stroke joins him with everything that has ever been painted in the world, without his having to leave either his place or time, or his blessed and accursed labor. The true history of painting is not one which puts painting in the past and then invokes superartists and fatalities—it is the history that puts everything in the present, that dwells in artists and reintegrates the painter with the fraternity of painters.

24. Translator: I think this is the sense of the text here.

Does this apply only to painters? Even if the innkeeper at Cassis does not understand Renoir's transmutation of the blue of the Mediterranean into the water of *The Bathers*, he wants to see Renoir at work. That *interests* him, too. And after all nothing prevents him from discovering that path which the cave dwellers one day opened without tradition. The world can become for him also a world to be painted. Renoir would have been quite wrong to ask his advice and try to please him. In this sense, he was not painting for the innkeeper. Through his painting, Renoir himself defined the conditions under which he intended to be approved. But ultimately he painted so that there would be a canvas there, *visible*. From the world, from the water of the sea, he redeemed the secret of the water in *The Bathers* and opened the path from the one to the other for those who, like himself, were caught up in the world. As Jules Vuillemin [25] says, it was not a question of speaking their language but of expressing them in expressing himself. With regard to his own life, the painter's attitude is of the same order: his style is not the style of his life, but he also draws his life toward expression.

It is understandable that Malraux does not like psychoanalytic *explanations* in painting. The explanation never goes far enough. Even if St. Anne's cloak is a vulture, even if one admitted that, while da Vinci painted it as a cloak, a second da Vinci in da Vinci, with his head tilted to one side, deciphered it as a vulture—like a reader of riddles (after all, it is not impossible: in da Vinci's life there is a frightening taste for mystification which could very well inspire him to enshrine his monsters in a work of art)—no one would speak about this vulture if da Vinci's painting did not have another meaning. The *explanation* accounts only for the details or at most for the materials in the work. Even if we admit that the painter likes to handle colors or the sculptor clay because he is an anal character, this does not always tell us what it is to paint or sculpt.[26] But the contrary attitude of the *devotion* to artists, which makes us not to want to

25. TRANSLATOR: Merleau-Ponty's successor to the chair of philosophy at the Collège de France.

26. Besides, Freud never said that he explained da Vinci by the vulture. He said in effect that analysis stops where painting begins.

know anything about their life and puts their work beyond private or public history and outside the world like a miracle, hides their true greatness from us. The reason that Leonardo is something more than one of the innumerable victims of an unhappy childhood is not that he has one foot in the great beyond but that he succeeded in making a means of interpreting the world out of everything he lived. It is not that he had no body or lacked sight, it is that he fashioned his corporeal or life situation into a language.

When one goes from the order of events to the order of expression, one changes levels but does not change the world. The *same* circumstances to which we first submitted now become a signifying system. Hollowed out, worked from within, and finally freed from that weight upon us which makes them painful, these circumstances become transparent or even luminous, capable of clarifying not only the aspects of the world which resemble them but the others too. However much they are transformed, they never cease to be there. The knowledge we may gain of them will never replace our experience of the work itself, although it helps us to evaluate the artistic creation. Here again the metamorphosis goes beyond circumstances while still preserving them, and the same tireless demand arises from every lived thing (at times trifling), namely, the demand to be expressed. Let us adopt *the painter's point of view* in the very moment where what he has to live as his corporeal destiny, his personal adventures or historical events, begins to crystallize in the act of painting, taking shape around certain vectors which indicate his fundamental relation to the world. Then we must recognize that his work, which is never an effect, is always a response to these circumstances. The landscapes, the schools, the mistresses, the creditors, the police, and the revolutions which may suffocate painting are also the bread the painter consecrates and the food which nourishes his painting. The painter is no longer isolated in a secret laboratory. To live through painting is still to breathe the air of this world. We must understand that the man who paints lives on the terrain of culture as "naturally" as if it had come from nature.

We should treat as "natural" even the relation the painter has to the history of painting. In his meditations upon miniatures and coins in which photographic enlargement miraculously reveals the very same style that is found in full-sized works—or upon those works of art from the Steppes which have been unearthed outside Europe, far from any influence, which astonish the moderns because they present the same style invented by a conscious painting or discovered by it elsewhere—Malraux is unable to avoid the idea of a "subterranean torrent" of history which reunites the most distant paintings, a Painting which works behind the painter's back, a reason in history of which he is the instrument. These Hegelian monstrosities are the antithesis and complement of Malraux's individualism. If one shuts up art in the secret reaches of the individual, one can explain the convergence of independent works only by some destiny which rules over them. But when, on the contrary, one puts painting back into the presence of the world, as we are trying to do, what becomes of Painting in itself or of the spirit of Painting?

Let us start with the simplest fact, which we have already clarified to some extent. We are surprised that the magnifying glass reveals the very same style in a medallion or miniature as the artists deliberately employed in full-sized works. But this is simply because, as we said earlier, our handwriting always has the same style whose movements are indivisible, so that we do not need to follow point by point the infinite path of the engraver who marked the material with its stripes. Our handwriting is recognizable whether we trace letters on paper with a pencil held by three fingers or on the blackboard with chalk held at arm's length—for our handwriting is more than simply a power that our body has of circumscribing a certain absolute space, limited once and for all by certain conditions and the use of certain muscles rather than others. It is a general capacity to formulate a constant type [of gesture?], handling all the transpositions that may be necessary.

Indeed, there is not even any transposition. We simply do not write in an object-space with an object-hand and an object-body for which each new situation presents problems. We write in a perceived space, where results with the same form are immediately analogous—if we ignore differences of scale—just as the same melody played at different pitches is immediately recognized. The hand with which we write is a hand-spirit [*main-esprit*] which, in the formula of a movement, possesses something like a natural concept of all the particular cases in which it may have to be operative. The whole miracle of a style already present in the invisible elements of a work or a miniature in the inhuman world is revealed by slow motion, the microscope, and the magnifying glass. This comes down to the fact that, working in the human world of perceived things, the artist comes to put his stamp upon even the inhuman world revealed by optical instruments—just as the swimmer unknowingly skims over a whole buried universe which would frighten him if he saw it with underwater goggles. Or like Achilles, in the simplicity of one step, the artist effects an infinite summation of spaces and instants.

There is no doubt that this is a great miracle whose strangeness should not be hidden from us by the word *man*. But we can at least recognize that this miracle is habitual and natural to us, that it begins with our incarnate life, and that there is no reason to seek its explanation in some spirit of the world which may work in us without our knowledge and think in our stead on a microscopic scale beneath the perceived world. Here, the spirit of the world is ourselves as soon as we know how *to move ourselves* and *to look*. These simple acts already contain the secret of expressive action. As the artist makes his style radiate into the very fibers of the material on which he is working, so I move my body without even knowing which muscles and nerve paths should intervene or where I should look for the instruments of this action. I want to go over there, and here I am, without access to the inhuman secret of the bodily mechanism, without having adjusted it to the objective requirements of the task or to the position of the goal defined in relation to some system of coordinates. I look where the goal is, I am drawn by it, and the whole bodily machine does what must be done for me to get there. Everything happens in the human world of perception and gesture, but my "geographical" or "physical" body obeys the requirements of this little drama which never ceases to produce a thousand natural miracles in my body.

My glance toward the goal already has its own miracles. It,

too, installs itself in being with authority and conducts itself there as in a conquered country. It is not the object which draws movements of accommodation and convergence (from the eyes). On the contrary, it has been demonstrated that I would never see anything clearly and that there would be no object for me, unless I used my eyes *in such a way as* to make the view of a single object possible. To complete the paradox, one cannot say that the mind takes the place of the body and anticipates what we will see. No, it is our glances themselves, their synergy, their exploration, and their prospecting which bring the immanent object into focus. The corrections would never be rapid and precise enough if they had to rely upon an actual calculation of effects. We must therefore recognize that what we call a "glance," a "hand," and in general the "body" constitute a system of systems devoted to the inspection of a world and capable of leaping over distances, piercing the perceptual future, and outlining, in the inconceivable platitude of being, hollows and reliefs, distances and gaps—in short, a meaning. . . . The movement of the artist tracing his arabesque in infinite matter amplifies but also prolongs the miracle of oriented motion or grasping movements. The body not only flows over into a world whose schema it bears in itself but possesses this world at a distance rather than being possessed by it. The gesture of expression which undertakes on its own account to delineate what it intends and make it appear outside, retrieves the world and remakes it in order to know it so much the more. But already, with our first oriented gesture, *someone's* infinite relationships to his *situation* had invaded our mediocre planet and opened an inexhaustible field to our behavior. All perception, and all action which presupposes it, in short, every human use of the body, is already *primordial expression.* This means that perception is not that derivative labor which substitutes for what is expressed in signs given elsewhere with their meaning and rule of use but the primary operation which first constitutes signs as signs. Perception makes what is expressed dwell in signs, not through some previous convention but through the eloquence of their very arrangement and configuration. It implants a meaning in what did not have one and thus, instead of exhausting itself in the moment it *occurs,* perception inaugurates an order and founds an institution or tradition.

Now, if the presence of style in miniatures which no one had ever seen, and in a sense no one had ever made, is compounded with the fact of our corporeality and does not call for any occult explanation, it seems to us that one can say as much of the singular convergences which all over the world make artists who are unaware of one another produce works that *resemble one another.* When we ask for a cause which explains these resemblances, we speak of a Reason in History, a Spirit of Painting, or a Superartist who guides artists without their knowing. But to begin with, to speak of *resemblances* is to put the problem badly. Resemblances are, after all, of little importance in terms of the innumerable differences and cultural variations. Thus when one encounters works which resemble one another from different continents or different centuries, the probability of rediscovery without any guide or model being involved is sufficient to account for the stylistic coincidence. The real problem is not to understand why works bear resemblances but why such different cultures become involved in the same search and set themselves the same task (and how, on this path, from time to time they encounter the same modes of expression). We must understand why what one culture produces has a meaning for another culture, even if it is not the original meaning—why we take the trouble to transform fetishes into art. In short, the true problem is to understand why there is a history of painting or a universe of painting.

However, this is a problem only if we have begun by placing ourselves in the geographical or physical world and by placing works of art there as so many events whose resemblance or mere connection then becomes improbable and calls for an explanatory principle. We propose, on the contrary, to consider the order of culture or meaning as an original order of advent which should not be derived from the order of mere events, if such exist, or treated simply as the effect of unlikely conjunctures. If it is characteristic of the human gesture to signify beyond its simple factual existence and to inaugurate a meaning, it follows that every gesture is *comparable* to all others. They all arise from a single syntax. Each gesture is both a beginning and a continuation which, insofar as it is not opaque and enclosed like an event that is complete once and for all, has a value beyond its simple presence and is in this respect allied in advance with or an accomplice in all other expressive efforts. Moreover, the human gesture is not only a possibility simultaneous with all other expressive efforts. It also assumes a structure with them in the world of painting. In addition, given that its trace remains and its heritage is transmitted, it is the essence of the pictorial gesture once made to modify the situation of the universal enterprise in which we are all engaged. Once the work is finished, it constructs new signs from signs, putting new significations at our disposal, and expands culture the way an additional organ might expand our bodily capacities. Thus it opens up a new research horizon. Likewise, all the gestures which constitute culture not only possess among them a principle of *affinity* which makes them elements in a single task; each demands the other in its difference, since there can be identical entities among them only insofar as they ignore each other. One is no longer surprised to find the artist's signature where his glance could not reach. In the same way, once one admits that the human body expresses itself in everything it does, so the convergences and correspondences between works of every kind that have no express influence on the history of art are not surprising from the standpoint of the order of culture as a unique field. We are not trying to say here that the human body provides an explanation * of this or that men who do not know each other, being separated by great stretches of time and space, revive the same gesture because they have the same body. It is precisely the character of the human body not to conduct itself on the basis of nature.

To be sure, the field of investigation inaugurated by a work may be abandoned if the work is lost, burned, or forgotten. The advent cannot dispense with events. There is no second causality above events which could make another suprasensible world from

* Nor is the permanence of the spirit the explanation. The real problem is not that of resemblances but that of the possibility of metamorphosis, of recapture. The resemblances are the exception. It is distinct to culture never to begin or finish at a given moment.

the world of painting—a world with its own laws, like the world of Grace about which Malebranche speaks. Cultural creation is ineffectual if it does not find a vehicle in external circumstances, for it can achieve nothing without them. But it is true that, if history is at all cooperative, a preserved painting handed on develops consequences in its inheritors which are out of all proportion to what it is as a piece of painted canvas. A unique history of culture knits together beneath the interruptions and regressions, because from the very beginning the original work had meaning beyond its empirical existence. The difficult and essential point here is to understand that in positing a field distinct from the empirical order of events, we are not positing a Spirit of Painting which is already in possession of itself on the other side of the world to which it then gradually reveals itself. . . . The order or field of significations which constitutes the unity of painting and in advance opens up each work to a future of investigations is comparable to the order the body opens up in its relation with the world wherein every gestural instance participates in the style of the whole.* Despite the diversity of its parts that makes it fragile and vulnerable, the body is capable of gathering itself into a gesture which for a time dominates the parts' dispersion and puts its stamp on everything it does. In the same way, we may speak of a unity of human style which transcends spatial and temporal distances to bring the gestures of all painters together in a single effort, a single accumulative history—a single art or culture.† The unity of culture extends beyond the limits of an individual life. The unity of culture is of the same sort as that which unites all the moments of an individual life once it is established—once, as we say, a consciousness is sealed in a body and there appears in the world a new being to whom anything can happen but to whom from now on

* The order of signifiers is comparable to that of the body. Acts of signification are essentially historical, the advent is event. The painter follows the course of perception. That does not mean that the body is the explanation.

† Naturally it is not a matter of the insertion of all painters in a single body: the body here is history. What is meant is that it exists *in the manner of* the body, that it is more like the body.

something cannot fail to pass and who must have a history, short or brief.

In its blindness to the perceived world, analytic thought breaks the perceptual transition from one place to another and from one perspective to another and then looks to the mind for the guarantee of a unity that is already given in perception. It also breaks the unity of culture and then tries to reconstitute it *ab extra*. After all, it says, there exist only works and individuals, how is it that they resemble one another? It is then that the Spirit of Painting is introduced. We must recognize as an ultimate fact our corporeal spanning of space and the body's power to bridge diversity, to see that our body, inasmuch as it is *alive* and makes itself gesture, relies only on itself and could never get its power from a separate spirit. In the same way, we must realize that the history of painting which runs from one work to another rests upon itself and is borne only by those efforts which knit together from the sole fact that they are attempts at expression. The intrinsic order of meaning is not eternal. Although it does not follow each zigzag of empirical history, it sketches out and calls for a series of successive steps. For it is not, as we have just stated provisionally, simply defined by the family relationship of all its moments within a single task. Precisely because they are all moments of painting, each painting, if it is preserved and transmitted, modifies the situation of the enterprise and for this reason requires that its successors be different. When we say that each [genuine?] work opens up an horizon of inquiry, we mean that it makes possible what was previously unavailable without it and that it transforms the pictorial enterprise while fulfilling it. Thus two cultural gestures can be identical only on the condition that they are unaware of one another. It is therefore essential to art to develop. Art must both change and, as Hegel says, "return to itself" and thus present itself as history. The meaning of the expressive gesture upon which we have based the unity of painting is in principle a meaning in genesis.

Advent does not leave time behind: it is a promise of events. The domination of the many by the one in the history of painting, such as we have met in the exercise of the perceiving body, does not consummate succession in an eternity. On the contrary, domination demands succession; domination needs succession at the same time that it grounds its signification. Between the two problems there is more than a simple *analogy*. It is the expressive operation of the body, begun in the least perception, which amplifies into painting and art. The field of pictorial significations was opened the moment a man appeared in the world. The first sketch on the walls of a cave founded a tradition only because it gleaned from another—the tradition of perception. The quasi eternity of art compounds the quasi eternity of our corporeal existence. It is through our body that we have the first experience of the impalpable body of history prior to all initiation into art.

In conclusion, let us point out that history understood in this way is saved from the empty discussions to which it is presently subject. History then becomes once again what it should be for the philosopher: the center of his reflections, not as an object-nature, absolutely clear in itself and the explanation of everything else, but on the contrary the place of all our questions and wonders. Whether they be an object of worship or of hate, today history and the dialectic of history are conceived as an external power. Consequently, we are forced to choose between this power and ourselves. To choose history means to devote ourselves body and soul to the advent of a future man and to renounce, in favor of this future, all judgments about means and all judgment about values or "self-consent to ourselves" for the sake of efficaciousness. This History-idol secularizes a rudimentary conception of God. It is no accident that contemporary discussions return so willingly to a parallel between what is called the "horizontal transcendence" of history and the "vertical transcendence" of God. In fact, this doubly misstates the problem. It is now more than two thousand years since Europe abandoned so-called vertical transcendence, and it is a little extravagant to forget that Christianity is for the most part the recognition of a mystery in the relation of man to God. This derives precisely from the Christian God's refusal of any vertical relation of subordination. He is not simply a principle of which we are the consequences, a will whose instruments we are. There is a sort of impotence of God without us. Claudel goes so far as to say that God is not above but beneath us—meaning that we find him not as a suprasensible model which we must follow but as another self in ourselves which dwells in and authenticates our darkness. Transcendence no longer hangs over man; strangely, man becomes its privileged bearer.

Furthermore, no philosophy of history has ever carried over all the reality of the present into the future or *destroyed* the self to make room for the future. Such a neurotic approach to the future would really be a nonphilosophy, the deliberate refusal to know *that in which one believes.* Hegel certainly does not introduce history as a brute necessity which obliterates judgment and suppresses the self; on the contrary, history is their true fulfillment. No philosophy has ever consisted in choosing between transcendences—for example, between that of God and that of a human future. Philosophies have all been concerned with mediating transcendences, with understanding how God makes himself man or how man makes himself God, or with elucidating that strange overlapping of means and ends which makes the choice of means already a choice of ends—making the justification of the means by the ends absurd. Or else philosophies have been concerned with how it is the self makes itself world or culture which in turn must be animated by the self. According to Hegel, as everyone repeats, all that is real is rational and thus justified. However, it is justified sometimes as a positive acquisition, sometimes as a pause, and sometimes as an ebbing withdrawal for a new surge. In short, all is justified relatively as a *moment* in total history on condition that this history makes itself and thus in the sense that our errors themselves are said to carry weight so that our progress is our mistakes understood—which does not erase the difference between growth and decline, birth and death, regression and progress. . . .

In his work on the concept of the state, Hegel departs from this wisdom.[27] But that is not a reason for forgetting that even in the *Philosophy of Right* he rejects, as errors of abstract understanding, both judging action by its results alone and judging action by its intentions alone. In the center of his thought is the

27. TRANSLATOR: *Hegel's Philosophy of Right*, trans. T. M. Knox (Oxford: Clarendon Press, 1942).

moment in which the internal becomes external, that turning or veering by which we merge with others and others in us. The polemics against "horizontal transcendence" in the name of "vertical transcendence" (admitted or simply regretted) are thus no less unjust toward Hegel than toward Christianity. The indigence of Marxist thought and the laziness of non-Marxist thought, each the other's accomplice as usual, today result in presenting the "dialectic" inside and outside us as a power of error, of falsehood and failure, the transformation of good into evil, the inevitability of deception. In Hegel, that was only one of the faces of the dialectic. It was also something like a grace which brought good from evil, for example, it thrusts us toward the universal when we think we are pursuing only our own interest. In itself, the dialectic was neither happy nor unhappy, neither the ruin of the individual nor the adoration of the future. It is, as Hegel says somewhere, *a movement which creates its own course and returns to itself*—and thus a movement with no other guide than its own initiative that nevertheless does not escape outside itself but cuts across its own path and confirms itself from cycle to cycle.

So the Hegelian dialectic is what we call the phenomenon of expression, which gathers itself step by step and launches itself again through the mystery of rationality. We would undoubtedly recover the true sense of the concept of history if we acquired the habit of modeling it on the example of the arts and language. The close connection between each expression and every other within a single order instituted by the first act of expression effects the junction of the individual and the universal. Expression—language, for example—is what most belongs to us as individuals, for while addressing itself to others, it simultaneously acquires a universal value. The central fact to which the Hegelian dialectic returns in a hundred ways is that we do not have to choose between the *pour soi* and the *pour autrui,* between our own version of thought and the version of others, which is alienation itself, because at the moment of expression the other to whom I address myself and I who express myself are linked without concession on either side. The others, such as they are or will be, are not the sole judges of what I do. If I wanted to deny myself for their benefit, I would deny them too as "self." They are worth exactly what I am worth, and all the powers I accord to them I give simultaneously to myself. I submit myself to the judgment of another who is *himself worthy of what I have attempted,* that is, in the last analysis, to the judgment of a peer whom I myself have chosen.

History is the judge—not History as the Power of a moment or of a century, but history as the space of inscription and accumulation beyond the limits of countries and epochs of what we have said and done that is most true and valuable, taking into account the circumstances in which we had to speak. Others will judge what I have done, because I painted the painting to be seen, because my action committed the future of others; but neither art nor politics consists in pleasing or flattering others. What they expect of the artist or politician is that he draw them toward values in which they will only later recognize their own values. The painter or politician shapes others more often than he follows them. The *public* at whom he aims is not given; it is a public to be elicited by his work. The others of whom he thinks are not empirical "others" or even *humanity* conceived as a species; it is others once they have become such [28] that he can live with them. The history in which the artist participates (and it is better the less he thinks about "making history" and honestly produces *his* work as he sees it) is not a power before which he must genuflect. It is the perpetual conversation woven together by all speech, all valid works and actions, each, according to its place and circumstance, contesting and confirming the other, each one re-creating all the others.

True history thus gets its life entirely from us. It is in our present that true history gets the force to refer everything else to the present. The *other* whom I respect gets his life from me as I get my life from him. A philosophy of history does not deprive me of any rights and privileges. It simply adds to my personal obligations the obligation to understand situations other than my own and to create a path between my life and the lives of others, that is, to express myself. The lines between one life and an-

28. EDITOR: Space in text.

other are not traced in advance. It is through the action of culture that I come to abide in lives that are not mine. I confront them, I reveal them to one another, I make them share equally in an order of truth. Responsible for all of them, I awaken a universal life—just as in one fell swoop I assume my place in space through the live and dense presence of my body. Like the operation of my body, the function of words or paintings remains obscure to me. The words, the lines, and the colors which express me come from me as my gestures and are torn from me by what I want to say the way my gestures are by what I want to do. In this sense, there is in all expression—even in linguistic expression—a spontaneity that will not tolerate commands, even those I would like to give to myself. In the art of prose, words carry the speaker and the listener into a common universe by drawing both toward a new signification through their power to designate in excess of their accepted definition or the usual signification that is deposited in them from the life they have had together in us. This is what Ponge very well described as the "semantic thickness" of words and Sartre as their "signifying soil." This spontaneity of language which saves us from conflicts is not a command. The history which it grounds is not an external idol. It is ourselves with our roots, our growth, and the fruits of our toil.

History, language, perception—only by bringing together these three problems can we put Malraux's fine analyses in proper perspective and draw their implicit philosophy from them. We shall then see how it is legitimate to treat painting as a language. This treatment will bring out in painting a *perceptual* meaning which is captured in the visible configuration of the painting yet able to gather up a series of antecedent sedimented expressions in an eternity always ready to be remade. It will also demonstrate that the comparison is useful not only for our analysis of painting but also for our analysis of language. For it will enable us to detect beneath spoken language, whose sounds and sentences are cleverly suited to ready-made significations, an operant or speaking language, whose words have a silent life like the animals at the bottom of the ocean and come together or separate according to the needs of their lateral or indirect signification. The transparency of spoken language, that fine clarity of the word which is nothing but its sound and of the meaning which is all meaning, speech's apparent property of extracting the meaning of signs to isolate that meaning in its pure state (in reality, the simple presumption of embodying the meaning in several formulae in which it would remain identical), and its alleged power of recapitulating and actually enclosing a whole process of expression in a single act—in short, this cumulative power of speech is only the highest point of a tacit and implicit accumulation of the same kind as that of painting.

We should begin by acknowledging that in most aspects language is not different from painting. A novel achieves expression the same way as a painting. One can discern the theme of a novel like that of a painting. But the virtue of the novel, like that of the painting, is not in the theme. What is important is not that Julien Sorel, after he has learned that he has been betrayed by Madame de Rénal, travels to Verrière and tries to kill her. It is that silence, that dreamlike journey, that thoughtless certainty, and that eternal resolution which follow the news. But there is no passage where these things are said. There is no need for "Julien thought" or "Julien wished." In order to express them, Stendhal had only to slip into being Julien, to enter a monologue within Julien, making objects, obstacles, means, and hazards flash before our eyes with the speed of the journey. He had only to decide to relate the journey in three pages instead of ten, to be silent about something rather than say such and such. It is not even that a novelist expresses *by choosing* the proportion between what he includes and what he omits. For him there is no question of choice. By consulting the rhythm of his own anger and his own sensibility to others, Stendhal suddenly endows them with an imaginary body more alive than his own. As though in a second life, he makes Julien's voyage according to the cadence of cold passion which selects for itself the visible and the invisible, what is to be said and what is to remain unsaid. The desire to kill is nowhere *in* the words. It is between them, in the hollows of space, time, and the significations they delimit, the way movement in the film is between the immobile images that follow one another, or the way the letters in some advertisements are made less by the few black lines than the white pages they vaguely indicate—blank, but full of meaning, vibrating with lines of force, as dense as marble. . . .

The novelist speaks to his reader—as every man does to another man—the language of the initiated, namely, those who are initiated into the world, to the universe of possibilities that belong to a human body and a human life. He assumes that what he has to say is known. He dwells in a character's behavior and gives the reader only a glimpse of it, a nervous and peremptory trace which it leaves on its surroundings. If he is a writer, that is, if he knows how to find the ellipses, elisions, and caesuras of conduct, the reader will respond to his appeal and meet him at the center of the imaginary world he animates and rules. The novel as a report of a certain number of events, as the promulgation of ideas, theses, or conclusions—in short, as direct, prosaic, or manifest signification, or the novel as the inauguration of a style, as oblique or latent signification—is in a simple relationship of homonymy. Marx clearly understood this when he adopted Balzac. To be sure, there is no question here of any return to liberalism. Marx meant that a certain way of bringing us to *see* the world of money and the conflicts of modern society was worth more than the *theses* on them and that this vision, once acquired, would have its right results with or without Balzac's consent.

It is certainly correct to condemn formalism, but it is usually forgotten that formalism's error is not that it overestimates form but that it esteems form so little that it abstracts it from meaning. In this regard formalism does not differ from a "thematic" literature which also separates the meaning and structure in a work. The true opposite of formalism is a good theory of speech which distinguishes speech from any technique or device. Speech is not a means in the service of an external end. It contains its own ebbing, its own rule of usage and vision of the world, the way a gesture reveals the whole truth about a man. This living use of language is the opposite of both formalism and "thematic" literature. Indeed, a language which aimed only at expressing things themselves would lose its power to instruct in factual statements. A language which, on the contrary, gives our perspective on things, thus putting things into relief, opens up a discussion over things which does not end with it but itself invites research and makes accumulation possible. What is irreplaceable in the work of art—what makes it not just a pleasant occasion but a voice of the spirit whose analogue is found in all productive philosophical or political thought—is that it contains, better than ideas, *matrices of ideas.* A work of art provides us with symbols whose meaning we shall never finish developing. Precisely because it comes to dwell in the world in which it makes us at home though we do not have the key to it, the work of art teaches us to see and makes us think as no analytic work can, because in the analysis of an object we cannot find anything other than what we have put into it.

What is hazardous in literary communication, or ambiguous and irreducible to a single theme in all the great works of art, is not a provisional weakness of literature which we could hope to overcome. It is the price we must pay to have a conquering language which, instead of limiting itself to pronouncing what we already know, introduces us to new experiences and to perspectives that can never be ours, so that in the end language destroys our prejudices. We would never see any new landscape if our eyes did not give us the means of catching, questioning, and shaping patterns of space and color hitherto unseen. We would not accomplish anything if our body did not enable us to leap over all the neural and muscular paths of locomotion in order to reach our projected goal. It is in the same brief imperious fashion and without transitions or preparations that we are thrown into a new world by the artist. Just as our body guides us among things only on the condition that we stop analyzing it in order to use it, so literary language can say new things only with the condition that we make common cause with it, that we stop examining its origins in order to follow where it is going, that we allow the words and means of expression in a book to be enveloped in that haze of signification that they derive from their particular arrangement, and finally, that we let the whole work veer toward a second-order tacit value where it almost rejoins the mute radiance of painting.

No less than with painting, the essential meaning of the

work of art is perceptible at first only as a *coherent deformation* imposed on the visible. It can never be otherwise. Critics may well compare one novelist's mode of expression with another's and incorporate one type of narrative in a family of other possible types or even of existing ones. . . . This is a legitimate task only if it relates differences of "technique" to differences in the over-all project and meaning. Above all, it must avoid the idea that to say *what* he had to say Stendhal could have borrowed Balzac's style and narrative. Critical thought explains us to ourselves in what we perceive in the novel and why we perceive it there. In place of the language of the novelist who shows or makes transparent what is true without touching it, criticism substitutes another language which claims to possess its object. But critical language is like one of those descriptions of a face in a passport which do not allow us to imagine the face. Critical thought takes the system of ideas and technical means which it finds in the work of art and abstracts them from the inexhaustible signification with which the novel is invested when it manages to throw our *image* of the world out of focus, to distend the dimensions of our experience and pull them toward a new meaning. Prior to any signification our experience is transformed when gripped by a novel, the way a figure acquires a new shape with the addition of an extra line.

Perhaps it will be replied that the aim of the critic's language, and especially of the philosopher's, is to convert into a solid possession the tenuous hold that literature has on experience. It remains to be seen—we shall examine this later—whether even in this case the critic and philosopher are not limited to an exercise, as it were of the second order and repetitive, of the same power of elliptical expression which creates the work of art. Let us begin, in any case, with the fact that at first sight philosophy does not, any more than art, engross its object, seizing it in its grip so as to leave nothing wanting. The transformations in Descartes's philosophy are famous. We explain him by the standards of our own understanding in the same way that modern painting classifies El Greco or Tintoretto. Before us, Spinoza, Malebranche, and Leibniz, as is well known, each in his own way put in the accents, altered the relations between "foreground" and "background," and defended his own Descartes. Descartes is, of course, that Frenchman who three centuries ago wrote the *Meditations* and other books, replied to Hobbes and Mersenne, took as his motto *larvatus prodeo,* and made the pilgrimage to Notre-Dame-de-Lorette. . . . But he is much more. Like Vermeer, Descartes is one of those institutions which are outlined in the history of ideas before they appear in person, as the sun can be seen before it suddenly unveils a renewed landscape. As long as these institutions last, they never cease to grow and to transform within themselves the events that confront them, until the movement begins imperceptibly to reverse itself and the situations and relations which the institutions cannot assimilate alter them and give rise to another form which, however, would not have been possible without them.

Descartes is Descartes. But he is also everything which seems to us after the fact to have prefigured him, to which he gave meaning and historical reality, as well as everything that derives from him, such as Malebranche's occasionalism hidden in the corner of the *Dioptics* and Spinoza's notion of substance in a digression in the *Reply to Criticisms.* How can we draw a line between Descartes's thought and what we have thought on the basis of it, between what we owe him and what we lend to him in our interpretations? To be sure, his successors stop where he moves quickly on and leave to oblivion what he was careful to explain, as though they were reorganizing the functions and vital centers of a great organism. But in the end it is still Descartes who awakens in them their own thoughts, who inspires their attack upon him. It is no more possible to make a strict inventory of the thoughts *of Descartes* than it is to inventory the means of expression in a language. Descartes conceived more clearly than anyone else the distinction between body and soul, and *for that very reason* he saw better than anyone else the paradox of their union in the practice of life. If one were to try to delimit Descartes not by his writings, which from the very beginning hum with the swarms of thoughts that were to invade them, but by what the man Descartes had in his head, noting each minute of his life, the summation would still not be possible. The field of our spirit, like our visual field, is not limited by any frontier; it runs out into a vague zone in which objects are outlined feebly but not without a kind of presence.

It is not simply because we lack information, because we have no dated diary of his thoughts, that we are unable to say whether or not at a given moment in his life Descartes conceived of idealism. It is because any thought that is at all profound sets in motion all the others, not just in writing but in the man's life. The movement of the second *Meditation* is and is not idealist, according to whether it is taken as *truth*—which, like all truth, cannot be surpassed and forces one to stop in it and dwell upon it forever, as Descartes himself wished—or, whether it is conceived as a partial truth which belongs to a larger truth that can be extrapolated to a divine author of the world, as Descartes also wished. The option one takes depends on whether one treats natural inclination as a particular case of the natural and inner light or makes the natural light an operation of the divine creator upon us. Since Descartes has on at least one occasion treated philosophy as meditation, we should not understand it as a movement of the spirit toward an external and immobile truth but as the transformation of thought's own certitudes and its own truth through the action of thought itself. This means that thought allows for the truth of each step which its conclusions validate and allows no truth that has not been *developed.* Thus, among other things, there is idealism in Descartes. But idealism as a moment is not idealism, and thus idealism is not in Descartes. But it is also there, since the other moments in which Descartes goes beyond idealism are not legitimate, because he exceeds it only by forgetting his starting point. . . .

Thus the discussion between commentators has its place. The inventory of thoughts formed by Descartes while he was alive is impossible, because of the principle that no thought can be separated by itself. There is idealism and no idealism in Descartes, just as in picture puzzles the rabbit is there in the foliage or he is not there, depending upon the angle of vision. The notion of a philosopher's thought apart from any ambiguity of texts, taken in itself (if that has any meaning), and its emergent state can be only a macroscopic phenomenon, since his thought is not a sum of ideas but a movement which leaves behind it a furrow as well as anticipating its future—in other words, the distinction between what is *to be found in it* and what future transformations will find in it. In comparing Descartes's works—the order of his thoughts, the words he uses, what he says firmly, and what he rejects—with Spinoza's works, one finds striking differences. But as soon as one goes beyond the external form of the texts and their common problem appears on the horizon, these erstwhile adversaries appear to be engaged in a more subtle struggle with one another, in which the parricide and the infanticide each strikes with the other's weapons. It is characteristic of cultural gestures to awaken in all others at least an echo if not a consonance. While Malebranche is writing to Dortous de Mairan everything he thinks bad about Spinoza, and those two opaque and obstinate minds are clashing, suddenly just where they lock together we no longer find two separate spirits each closed in himself and alien to the other. We find that in striking the other each hurts himself. It is no longer a matter of an individual struggle but of a tension in the Cartesian world between essence and existence.

We are not trying to introduce any skeptical conclusion here. It is only within the same Cartesian world that the adversaries are brothers, and they are not unwitting relatives. Malebranche is so hard on Spinoza only because Spinoza is able to push him far down the road to Spinozism, toward which he does not want to travel. Thus we are not saying that all opposition is useless or that some Providence in things makes the whole world right. We are saying that in the same cultural world everyone's thoughts lead a hidden life in the others, as a kind of obsession, each being moved by the other and entangled with him the moment he begins to offer resistance. This is not a skeptical principle; on the contrary, it is a principle of truth. We really inhabit the same world and are open to truth precisely because there arises this diffusion among thoughts, this osmosis which makes the cloistering of thought impossible and deprives of all meaning the question of *to whom* a thought *belongs*. Finally, if, unable to find the absolute truth of Descartes in his written works or lived thoughts, we were to seek it in the undivided choice which underlay not just these works and his favorite thoughts but also his daily adventures and actions, we would indeed come to the depths of the individual, to what "a thousand years of history cannot destroy." [29] In saying yes or no to whatever was given him to see, to know, or to live, Descartes's irrevocable decisions set a "limit" that no future can break down and thus define, one would think, the absolute with respect to Descartes that cannot be altered by any metamorphosis. Nevertheless, the question is not to know whether someone said yes or no but why he did, what meaning he attached to the yes or no, what it was he accepted, and what exactly he refused. Among his contemporaries Descartes's decisions had to be understood and they managed to do so only in the light of their own. Descartes himself was unable, in his own eyes, to define himself through his deeds. He could neither vanish behind his decisions nor reduce himself to them. He too had to discern their underlying project and the meaning he gave them. Each decision had only a provisional meaning and needed those that followed to give it a determinate sense.

The proof of the *se esse*, which the *Rules* include among the simple natures, had to be separated from them in the *Meditations* as a primary truth and a privileged experience. The meaning of the *se esse* in the *Rules* was therefore suspended. Since one can say the same thing of all the other works of Descartes, and since a philosopher either stops writing or dies—not because his work is finished but because beneath his total project of living and thinking something is suddenly missing—and since every death is premature from the point of view of the mind it strikes, the life and entire work of Descartes acquire a final irrevocable meaning only in the eyes of his survivors, through the illusion of the alien spectator. While he was alive, each decision for Descartes himself had to be interpreted in terms of his other decisions, however one pressed him to declare himself within his historical horizon and in the face of whatever institution, whether the dominant philosophy or the ruling religion, and however resolutely he said yes to this or no to that. The question of Descartes's religion is not settled by the pilgrimage to Notre-Dame-de-Lorette or by what he says about Catholicism in his works. It remains to

29. Jean-Paul Sartre.

be known what this yes *may be,* when taken with the rest of his expressed thoughts. It is not a matter so much of knowing *whether* he was a believer as of knowing the sense in which he was and the function of religion in the whole of Descartes's life. Was it present in him only in a marginal fashion, anonymously, like a component of the historical makeup of his time, and without compromising the real center of his thought as seen in the natural light? Or did it, on the contrary, reach the very heart of Descartes's philosophy—and, if so, how did it fit with the rest? We should not *postulate* that these questions which our interpretation raises were ever even articulated by Descartes or resolved by him the day he decided to make the pilgrimage to Notre-Dame-de-Lorette and that he withheld the answer in some secret depths which would contain the absolute truth of Descartes. No less obscure in his own eyes than ours, Descartes could act as though he did not have the key to his own life. Possibly, having been born when religion was established, he simply joined in the general religion and combined in himself its beliefs and a natural light discordant to us, without seeking any common center to them. Finally, perhaps there is no single key to Descartes's life. It may seem enigmatic only in the same way as do the irrational, the pure fact, the inherence of a mind into a particular time—in other words, enigmatic in itself, without any solution's existing. . . .

Whether the key to Descartes lies in religion or pure thought, his own secret was not given to him ready made. No less than ourselves he had to decipher or discover it. This interpretative effort is what we call his work and life. It is because he is long dead that it is we who imagine an absolute Descartes, as he was in his time, hard as a diamond, with his concrete tasks, his decisions, and his enterprises. For himself, in his present he cannot do other than produce every minute a signification "Descartes," with everything that is questionable in significations. He cannot make a gesture without entering the labyrinth of Cartesian interpretation and waiting for the others to meet him there. He has hardly to refer to the singular juncture of circumstances which constitute his historical milieu—his teaching at the college of La Flêche, geometry, philosophy as he inherited it from his predecessors, the war which he was to join, the servant who was to give him a daughter, that terrible Queen of Sweden whom he had to instruct—and under his fingers everything acquires the meaning of Descartes. Whatever may be understood in several senses, all begins to function in the world of Descartes. He is as enigmatic as any individual. His own life begins to testify to a way of treating life and the world. Like any other, this testimony must be interpreted. We cannot find even in the total individual that *essence of Descartes* that we vainly sought in his thought, or, rather, we find it only as an enigma without being sure there is any answer to the enigma. What accounts for the fact that this life which ended three centuries ago has not been buried in Descartes's tomb, and so remains a symbol and a text for us all to read, lying there "unarmed and unconquered, like a boundary stone," is precisely that it was already signification and in this sense called for a metamorphosis. Then it would be useless to look even here for something that did not belong to Descartes. He is not an individual in the manner of a stone or an essence. He is singular like a tone, a style, or a language, that is, he can be shared by others and is more than just singular. Even when related to his life, the philosopher's thought—the more determined it is to be explicit, to define itself, and to distinguish itself—remains, like the allusive thought of the novelist, unable to express itself without hints.

It is still true that language, even if in fact it relapses into the precariousness of mute forms of expression, has in principle other intentions.

The man who speaks or writes takes an attitude toward the past which is his alone. The whole world and its civilizations continue the past. Today's parents see their childhood in their own childrens' and adopt toward them their own parents' attitudes. Or, out of rancor, they go to the opposite extreme. If they have had an authoritarian upbringing, they practice a permissive one. But through this detour they often return to their tradition. In twenty years the dizziness of freedom will swing the child back to a system of security and make him an authoritarian father. All our behavior toward a child is perceived by him not only in terms of its effects but also of its principle. He not only submits to it as a child but assumes it as a future adult. The child is not only an object but already a subject in complicity with the experiences to which he submits because his father is another version of himself. Therefore authoritarian education does not, as is believed, lead to rebellion. After the rebellion of youth one sees the same image of one's father reappear in the adult. Perhaps this is because, with extraordinary subtlety, the child sees not just his parents' rigidity but behind it the depth of anguish and uncertainty which often motivate it. In suffering the one he learns also to suffer the other. When he becomes a parent he will escape from neither and will enter on his own account into the labyrinth of anguish and aggression which makes us violent. Thus, despite zigzags which sometimes go full circle, every little man, through every concern of which he is the object and every gesture that he witnesses, identifies with his parents' way of life. He builds up a passive tradition in which the whole weight of experience and his own achievements will hardly be enough to introduce a small change. This is the way that formidable and necessary integration of culture, the grip from age to age of destiny, accumulates. Of course, changes intervene, if only because the child inherits conclusions without having lived the premises. Thus behavior that has been learned apart from the experiences which motivated it can be invested with a new meaning. But in any case, these changes are made in obscurity. The child rarely understands his race or the profound emotions from which he has begun to live. He rarely draws an education from them instead of letting them play on him. Usually he is content to continue them not in their truth but in what is injurious and intolerable in them. On the surface, a culture's tradition is orderly and monotonous; underneath there are chaos and tumult, and even the break from tradition is no more a liberation than docility.

The immense novelty of expression is that in the end it makes tacit culture leave its mortal circle. When the arts appear in a culture, a new relation to the past also appears. An artist is not content to continue the past out of reverence or revolt. He begins it again. He cannot childishly believe that his life is made for prolonging the lives of others. If he takes up the brush, it is because in one sense painting still remains to be created. Yet this very independence is suspect. Precisely because painting always remains to be taken up, the works he will produce will be *added* to works already done which they neither contain nor make useless but renew. Today's painting, even though it was possible only through the whole past of painting, denies this past too deliberately really to be free of it. Today's painting can only forget the past. The ransom it pays for its novelty is that, in making what came before it seem to be an unsuccessful effort, it foreshadows another painting which tomorrow will make it in its turn appear to be unsuccessful. Thus painting as a whole presents itself as an abortive effort to say something which still remains to be said. Here we can see what is characteristic of language.

The author who is not content to carry on in the language he inherited or to repeat what has already been said still does not want, any more than the painter, to replace it with an idiom which is self-sufficient and closed within its own signification. He wants to fulfill language and destroy it at the same time, to fulfill it *by destroying it* or to destroy it *by fulfilling it*. He destroys it as ready-made language which awakens in us only half-dead significations and does not convey the life of what it is saying. He fulfills it because language as it is penetrates him through and through and already offers a general outline of his most secret thoughts and, rather than confront him as an enemy, it is entirely *ready* to convert into an acquisition the new signification he creates. It is as though language had been made for him and he for language; as if the task of speaking assigned to him by language and to which he was devoted while learning it was more himself than his own heartbeat—or as if institutionalized language already contained the writer as one of its own possibilities. Each new painting occurs in the world inaugurated by the first painting. It fulfills the vow of the past; it has the past's proxy and acts in its name. But it does not contain the past in a manifest state and is a memory for us only if we also know the history of painting. It is not a memory in itself and does not pretend to summarize all that made it possible.

Speech, on the other hand, is not content to go further but pretends to recapture, recover, and contain the substance of the past. Since speech cannot yield the living past unless it repeats the past textually, speech makes the past undergo a preparation that enables the past to reveal itself in speech: speech wants to give us the *truth* of the past. Speech knits to itself, resumes itself, and regathers itself. Speech is not content to push the past to make place in the world for itself. Speech wants to conserve the past either in its spirit or in its meaning.

The properties of the fraction do not falsify the whole number. The same is true of the relation between spatial geometry and plane geometry, non-Euclidean geometry and Euclidean, or Einstein's concepts and those of classical physics. The new formulations make the old ones specially simple cases in which certain possible variations have not been utilized and would be wrong only if one pretended to grasp being itself through them. Plane geometry is the geometry of a space where there is a single null dimension, and Euclidean space is a space of n dimensions in which there are $n - 3$ null dimensions. Thus the truth of ancient formulations is not an illusion. They are false in what they reject but true in what they affirm. It is possible only *ex post* to see the anticipation of the explanations to follow. It is thus characteristic of the algorithm to conserve ancient formulae to the extent that it converts them to themselves and their legitimate meaning, reconfirming them at the same time it supersedes them, saving them by destroying them, and thus making them appear as elements in a developing whole or as samples of a future ensemble.

In all these cases, sedimentation is not only the accumulation of one creation upon another but also an integration. The first steps do not merely launch a vague appeal to the future. The future realizes a consummation which is the very one for which the first steps called, since it saves them. Thus they are the experience of the same truth in which they will be grounded. That is how science accumulates, whereas painting is always in suspense. That is the way the algorithm makes available the significations it yields, that is, by making them appear to us to have an independent life beyond their provisional formulations. There is thus something analogous in all languages. The writer can conceive of himself only in an established language, whereas every painter refashions his language. This means a great deal. It means that the literary work seeks reincorporation in the common good which language constitutes. It also means that the literary work conceives itself from the beginning as contained within language, at least in principle, and that the very transformations it introduces remain recognizable after the writer is gone, whereas the painter's experience ceases to be identifiable once it passes into his successors. It means that the past of language is not just a dominated past but also an understood past. Painting is unable to speak.

There is a critical, philosophical, and universal use of language which claims to retrieve things as they are—whereas painting transforms them into painting—to retrieve everything, both language itself and the use other doctrines have made of it. Socrates kills Parmenides, but philosophical murders are simultaneously the recognition of a filiation. Spinoza thinks he is expressing the truth of Descartes. Hegel, of course, thinks he expresses the truth of Descartes, Spinoza, and all the rest. But without our giving further examples, it is evident that the moment he seeks the truth the philosopher does not think that it had to wait for him to be true. He pursues it as what has always been true for everyone. It is essential that truth be integral, whereas no painting has ever pretended to be. If the unity of styles, as Malraux says, appears only in the Museum where there is a *comparison* of works—if it lies *between* or behind the paintings to the point where the Museum makes styles appear like "superartists" behind artists and the history of painting look like a subterranean glow whose energy none of the styles can exhaust—that is because the Spirit of Painting is a spirit extended to itself. For language, on the contrary, it is essential to pursue self-possession, to master through criticism the secret of its own inventions of style, to talk about speech instead of only using it. In a word, the spirit of language is or pretends to be spirit for itself, to have nothing that does not come from itself.

The attitudes of language and painting with regard to time are almost opposite. Despite the dress of the characters, the forms of the furniture and utensils in a painting, and the historical circumstances to which it can allude, a painting establishes its charm from the start in a dreaming eternity to which we may easily return many centuries later, even without having been initiated in the civilization where it originated. Writing, however, begins to communicate its most lasting sense to us only after it has introduced us to circumstances and arguments long since past. The *Provincial Letters* would tell us nothing if they did not bring the theological disputes of the seventeenth century back into the present. *The Red and the Black* would tell us nothing without the gloom of the French Revolution. But painting pays curiously for its immediate access to permanence which it grants itself, for it is subject much more than writing to the passage of time. Even Leonardo da Vinci's masterpieces make us think of him rather than ourselves and of Italy rather than men. Literature, on the contrary, insofar as it renounces the hypocritical prudence of art and bravely confronts its times—displaying them, rather than vaguely evoking them—"grounds them in signification" forever. Sophocles, Thucydides, and Plato do not reflect Greece, they make Greece visible even to us who are so distant from it. The Olympian statues, which do as much if not more to attach us to Greece, in the state in which they have come down to us—bleached, broken, fragments torn from a whole work—foster a fraudulent myth about Greece. They cannot resist time the way a manuscript does. Even when torn, almost illegible, and reduced to a few phrases, a manuscript can throw more light for us than any broken statue, because its signification lies and is concentrated in a different way than in stones, and because nothing equals the ductility of speech. The first painting opens up a world, but the first word opens up a universe. In short, language *speaks*, and the voices of painting are the "voices of silence."

If we press the meaning of the little word "say" and bring into the light what constitutes the price of language, we would find that it is the intention to unveil the thing itself and to go beyond what is said to what what is said signifies. It does not help for every word to refer back to all other possible words for its meaning, because the very moment the word is produced the task of expression can no longer be differentiated or returned to other words—it has been uttered and we understand something. Following Saussure, we said earlier that a single act of speech is not significant by itself but only as a modulation of a general system of expression and insofar as it is *differentiated* from other linguistic gestures of which language is composed. Language is more than simply the vehicle of a sum of differences in significations. It presupposes a general communication, however vague and unarticulated. We should now note that the marvel is that we knew nothing about this before Saussure, and that we forget it each time we speak—for example, when we speak about Saussure. The marvel is that this simple power of differentiating significations which it cannot give to what does not have them, namely, speech, nevertheless seems to contain and carry significations within it. This means we should avoid the vicious circle of deducing the signifying power of each word from others or even from a global power of language. A whole may have other properties than its elements but it is not created *ex nihilo.* Each partial linguistic act, as an act common to the whole of the given language, is not limited to expending its expressive power but re-creates that power by making us verify, through the evidence of given and received meaning, the power that speaking subjects have of going beyond signs toward their meaning—of which what we call language is, after all, only the visible result and record. Signs do not simply evoke other signs for us and so on endlessly. Language is not like a prison into which we are locked or a guide whose directions we must follow blindly. For in their everyday use, what signs mean appears at the intersection of all those thousands of signs to which they lead us so easily that we no longer need them to be able to refer back to their meaning. It may well be that in the end we realize that we have not reached the things themselves and that this halt in the volubility of our spirit occurred only to prepare for a new departure. Similarly, Euclidean space, far from possessing an ultimate clarity, still has the opacity of a very special case, and its truth proves to be only of a second order which must be grounded in a new generalization of space. All the more is it the case that the movement by which we pass from a naïve to a less naïve evidence establishes between the one and the other a relation of implication which is characteristic of things said.

The schizophrenic and the philosopher each knocks himself

against the paradoxes of existence. As a result each consumes his energy in amazement and, we may say, fails to recapture completely the world. But not to the same extent. The schizophrenic is ruled by his failure which expresses itself only in a few enigmatic phrases. What we call the philosopher's failure leaves behind him a whole furrow of expressive acts which enable us to rediscover our situation. Thus in comparing language to mute forms of expression—to gesture and painting—we should not overlook the point that language, unlike them, is not content to draw lines, vectors, a "coherent deformation," or tacit meaning on the surface of the world. The chimpanzee who learns to use a branch to reach his goal ordinarily does so only if the two objects can be seen in a single view, if they are within "visual contact." This means that the *new meaning* of the branch is a bundle of practical intentions which join it to the chimpanzee's goal. The meaning lies in the immanence of a gesture, that is, in the index of the manipulation. The new meaning is born in the circuit of desire between the chimpanzee's body and what it seeks; the branch happens to break into this circuit only insofar as it facilitates it; the branch does not retain all its properties as a branch. The psychologists have shown that to a chimpanzee a box is either something to sit on or something to climb on but not both at the same time. Once he sees another chimpanzee sitting on the box, the chimpanzee will stop climbing on it. This means that the signification which develops in objects is viscous. It adheres to their fortuitous distribution and is a signification only for a body engaged at a given moment in a given task.

However, when we grasp the signification of language it seems to be free from any task it accomplishes. To find the area of a parallelogram, I treat it as a possible triangle and dictate the properties which are deducible in terms of this transformation. I do not limit myself by changing the object. Instead, I posit that these changes in the parallelogram leave the object intact and that in the parallelogram itself, insofar as it is a virtual triangle, the area is equal to the product of the base times the height. This is not just a substitution of one meaning by another but a substitution of *equivalent meanings*, in which the new structure appears latent in the old one while remaining present in the new. The past is not simply surpassed, it is *understood*—which is what we express in saying that there truth exists and that here spirit emerges. A moment ago, as in a kaleidoscope, a new landscape was suddenly offered to the animal's action, given certain factual conditions from which he profited. Now, the same object reveals a property that is its own, which it had before us and will retain afterward. We have moved from the realm of causes to the realm of reasons and from a temporality that accumulates change to a temporality which understands them.

Nevertheless, we must see that we do not always escape from time or a certain field of thought. Even he who understands geometry is not always a mind without any situation in the natural and cultural world. He is the inheritor and at best the founder of a certain language whose signification does not transcend the *factual presence* of its signs, a language which, like an institution, is beyond the contingencies from which it arose. Of course, when Galileo succeeded in bringing under one signification the factors of uniform acceleration and deceleration—for example, the stone thrown in the air and the uniform rectilinear movement of a body on which there is no impinging force—these phenomena became variants of a single dynamic. Then it appears to us that he had fixed an *essence* of which the examples are only *examples*. But this signification can in principle appear only through the concrete shapes which it unifies. That it appears to us on the basis of "particular cases" is not an accident of its genesis with no essential effect. The signification is inscribed in its content, and if we tried to abstract the signification from the circumstances in which it appears, the signification would vanish before our eyes. The latter is not so much a signification over and above the facts which signify it as our means of passing from one fact to another or the trace of their intellectual generation.

The truth that is unique and common and afterward seems to us to have emanated from the facts does not lie *behind them* the way reality is behind appearances. That truth cannot found any progressive movement from which we could deduce appearances, for it is *their* truth only provided we always maintain contact with them. When Gauss remarks that the sum of the *n* prime numbers is equal to $\frac{n}{2}$ partial sums, so that is equal to $n + 1$, and concludes with the formula $\frac{n}{2}(n + 1)$ which applies to a whole continuous series of numbers, what convinces him that he has found the essence and truth is that from this series he can *see* the derivation of the constant values he will reckon instead of calculating their sum. The formula $\frac{n}{2}(n + 1)$ contains the essence of this mathematical fact and is demonstrated only insofar as we understand, under each use of the sign n, the double function it fulfills, namely, as the number of figures to be summed (n ordinal) and the final number of the series (n cardinal). Any other equivalent algebraic formula which we may deduce from this one, such as $\frac{n + 1}{2}(n)$ or $n\frac{(n + 1)}{2}$ or $\frac{n^2 + n}{2}$, has expressive value only through its intermediary because only the intermediary can make visible the relation between the object considered and its "truth." Of course, a blind thought could use the latter formulae and the results achieved would *also* be true, but only to the extent we could reconstruct them from the formula by repeating the operation that enabled us to construct the results from the series of numbers.

Thus nothing limits our power to formalize, that is, to construct increasingly general expressions of the same fact. But however far one proceeds with formalization, its signification remains in suspension, actually means nothing, and has no truth at all unless we refer its superstructures back to a visible object. To signify, to signify something as a decisive act, is therefore accomplished only when that something's constructions are applied to the perceived as the source of signification or expression. The perceived object, with its viscous significations, has a twofold relation to what is understood. On the one hand, it is only the sketch or fragment of meaning which calls for a repetition that fixes the perceived object and finally makes it *exist*. On the other, the perceived object is the prototype of meaning and alone accomplishes the actual truth of what is understood. To be sure, if we are to understand the sensible as quality, it must contain everything we think, although almost nothing in human perception is entirely sensible, since the sensible is indiscoverable. But there is also nothing that we can actually and effectively think without relating it to our field of presence, to the actual existence of the perceived object—and in this sense the field of presence contains everything. There is no truth that can be conceived only outside the field of presence, outside the limits of some situation or some structure. We are able to sublimate this situation to make it appear a particular case in a family of situations, but we cannot cut the roots which implant us in a situation. The formal transparency of the algorithm recaptures a back-and-forth operation between sensible structures and their expression as well as the whole genesis of intermediary significations—but must we reactivate them to think the algorithm?

Although it is characteristic of sedimentation in the sciences to contract a series of operations in the evidence of a single formula which no longer needs to be made explicit for us to work with it, the structure so defined keeps its full sense and capacity for new developments of knowledge only if it retains some relation to our experience and if we begin again, even if by a shorter route, to reconstruct it from this basis. It is we who say that superseded theories are conserved in later ones. But we do so only by means of a transposition which makes transparent the obscurity that affects theories as much as facts. The errors of superseded truths are salvaged only as truths and thus they are not salvaged. Perhaps it is through these errors that theory, apart from its own claims and evidence, leaves a fringe of anticipated knowledge which science at its next turn will pursue. Valid science is built not just upon its present but also upon its past.

If this is true of the algorithm, it is all the more true of language. Hegel is the only one who thinks that his system contains the truth of all the others, and anyone who knew the others only through Hegel's synthesis would not know them at all. Even if Hegel's entire body of work were true, we could not dispense with reading his predecessors, for he can contain them only "in what they affirm." By what they deny, they offer the reader another situation of thought which is not eminently contained in Hegel—which is not there at all—and in which Hegel is visible in a light of which he himself is unaware. Hegel is the only one to think he has no existence for the other and that he appears in the other's eyes just as he is known to himself. Even if his work represents a progression with respect to other philosophies, it is possible for there to have been, in a given passage from Descartes or Plato, in a section of the *Meditations* or the *Dialogues*—precisely because of the "naïvetés" which still separated them from the Hegelian "truth"—a contact with things and a spark of meaning that can be found in the Hegelian synthesis only on the condition that we continuously return to them, if only for the sake of understanding Hegel himself. Hegel is the museum. He is all philosophies, if you like, but without their shadowy zone, their finitude, and their lively impact, as he believed, embalmed and transformed into themselves but really transformed into Hegel. We have only to see how a truth wastes away when it ceases to stand alone and is integrated into a larger truth—how, for example, the *cogito*, in passing from Descartes to Malebranche, to Leibniz, or even to Spinoza, ceases to be a thought and becomes a conceptual ritual reeled off the tip of the tongue—to understand that the synthesis cannot on pain of death be an objective synthesis which would effectively contain all past systems of thought. It cannot be a real synthesis either, one which *would be* everything that earlier systems have been. Finally, it cannot be a synthesis in and for itself which *at the same time and in the same respect* is and knows, is what it knows, knows what it is, preserves and suppresses, destroys and fulfills.

Hegel tells us that the synthesis retains the past "in its present profundity." But how does the synthesis have a profundity and in what does that profundity consist? It is the profundity of that which the synthesis no longer is, the profundity of the past, and it is not true thought which engenders the past, for it is initiated into the past only through the fact of the past or through the passage of time. Let us assume that Hegel means that this passage is not a simple destruction. As it becomes distant the past changes into its meaning. At an equal distance from an order of unchanging natures and the circulation of the moments of time which chase after each other, we are able afterward to trace an intelligible history and revive the past in our living present. If this is Hegel's meaning, then he is right—but on condition that this synthesis, like the one yielded to us by the perceived world, remains on the order of the preobjective and is disputed by each of the terms it unites. Rather, it is on condition that each of the terms remains in its present state and equal to the whole, that is, the whole of the world at a particular date, and that the linkage of philosophies in an intentional history remains a confrontation of open significations, an exchange of anticipation and metamorphosis.

There is no doubt that in a certain sense the least student of philosophy today thinks with fewer prejudices than Descartes. In this sense he is nearer to the truth. This claim could be made by anyone who tangles with thought after Descartes. Nevertheless, it is Descartes who thinks through his descendants, and what we can say against him is still only the echo of his brief and determined speech. It is through the others that we understand Hegel, even where he surpasses them, just as much as we understand them through him. A present which actually contained the past in the whole of its meaning as past, and in particular the past of all the pasts, the world in all the meaning of the world, would also be a present without a future, since it would no longer have any reserve being in which something could happen to it. The cruel idol of the Hegelian *l'en-soi-pour-soi* is precisely the definition of death. Sedimentation is not the end of history. There is no history if there remains nothing of what passes and if each present in its very singularity does not inscribe itself once and for all in the tableau of what has been and continues to be. However, there is no history unless this tableau is carved out in terms of a temporal perspective, unless the meaning which appears in it is the meaning of a genesis which is accessible to a mind open in the same way the genesis was. Here the height of wisdom and of cunning is a profound naïveté.

As for literature, it is ordinarily more resolute in accepting that it can never aim at being total and offering us only open significations. Mallarmé himself knew very well that nothing would come from his pen if he remained absolutely faithful to his vow to say *everything* and that he was able to write books only by giving up The Book—or, rather, that The Book could be written only as several books. Every writer knows too well that language yields nothing more than we ourselves find in it and that there is no golden age of language. Once he has received a language in which he will write, everything remains to be done. He must remake *his* language within this language, which provides him only with an external signaling of things. His desired contact with things does not lie in the beginning of language but at the end of language's effort. In this sense, the existence of a given language masks from us more than it reveals of the true function of speech. When we contrast the eloquence of language with the silence of painting, we usually compare classical language and modern painting. If we were to contrast the modern writer's language with the apparent eloquence of classical painting, perhaps the result would be the opposite—we could find beneath the rigidity of the classical painters their tacit profundity. Once again, painting and language would appear equal in the prodigy of expression.

It is true that not all men paint, whereas all painters speak—and more than is required by life's needs or even their painting. Man feels *at home* in language the way he never will in painting. Ordinary language or the givens of language provide him with the illusion of an absolutely transparent expression which has achieved its goal. But in the end art itself also passes into custom and becomes capable of the same ingrained evidence. After a time, art becomes generalized. Then what remains of surrealism in our shop windows is worth about what remains of Plato in Aristotle or of Descartes in Hegel. If it is legitimate to credit the activity of language not only with languages but also with speech, to be just we should also credit the activity of painting not only with registered acts of expression, namely, paintings, but also with the continued life of its past in the painter at his work. The inferiority of painting would then be due to its registering only in works and not entering the foundations of the everyday relations between men, whereas the life of language which uses ready-made words from a sonorous material in which we are all rich yields a [perpetual?] commentary on spoken language.

We are not disputing what belongs to sedimentation characteristic of language, namely, the power of critical forms of language, if not to detach significations from signs or the concept from the linguistic gesture, at least to find for the same signification several expressive embodiments, to blend and recapture through one another its successive or simultaneous operations, and thus to combine them in a single configuration and a single truth. All we are saying is that, although this system displaces the center of gravity in our life and institutes, as far as anything we can read, an instance of truth whose consequence cannot be limited—which makes painting appear to be a "mute" and subordinate form of expression—it still does not escape the limits that define sensible expression. It only carries them further. We are saying that the "natural light" which discovers the system is the same as that which makes the meaning of a painting visible and yet recaptures the world no more than the painting does. Thus once language has become sufficiently self-conscious to have a view of itself, once it seeks paradoxically to designate and name the signification without any sign whatsoever (which it believes to be the height of clarity but which would extinguish it), indeed, what Claudel calls "sigè l'abîme" [30]—then language would have to forsake being the Parmenidean sphere or the transparence of a crystal with simultaneously visible sides and return to the cultural world, with that world's identifiable facets but also with its fissures and gaps.

We must therefore say about language in relation to meaning what Simone de Beauvoir says of the body in relation to mind: it is neither primary nor secondary. One does not love by means of principles. Though there have been philosophers to make eulogies of marriage instead of love, at least they have not tried to define love in terms of marriage. Thus no one has ever dared really to place the soul in the body, like a pilot in his ship, or to make the body into an instrument. Furthermore, since it is not the body alone which loves (the body snatches from those who want to live from it alone gestures of tenderness that go far beyond the

30. TRANSLATOR: "Time is the means offered to all that which will be, in order to be no more. It is the *Invitation to Death* extended to each sentence, to decay in the explanatory and total harmony, to consummate the word of adoration whispered in the ear of Sigē, the Abyss" (Paul Claudel, *Poetic Art,* trans. Renee Spodheim [New York: Philosophical Library, 1948], p. 35). Σιγή is silence.

body), the body is and is not ourselves. The body does everything and it does nothing. Neither end nor means, always involved in matters which go beyond it, always jealous of its autonomy, the body is powerful enough to oppose itself to any merely deliberate end yet has none to propose to us if we finally turn toward and consult it. Sometimes—and then we have the feeling of being ourselves—the body really lends itself to what we want, allowing itself to be animated, and takes on a life which is more than its own. Then the body is happy and spontaneous and so are we. Similarly, language is not the servant of meaning and does not govern meaning. There is no subordination or anything but a secondary distinction between them. Here no one commands and no one obeys. In speaking or writing, we do not refer to some *thing to say* which is before us, distinct from any speech. What we have to say is only the excess of what we live over what has already been said. We set up our abode with our linguistic apparatus in a certain situation of knowledge and history to which that apparatus is sensitive, and our pronouncements are only the final balance of these exchanges.

Despite appearances, political thought is of the same order. It is always the elucidation of a historical perception in which all our understandings, all our experiences, and all our values simultaneously come into play—and of which our theses are only the schematic formulation. All action and knowledge which do not go through this elaboration, but seek to impose *ex nihilo* values that have not been drawn from our individual and collective history, which would make the calculations of means a completely technical thought process, reduce knowledge and practice below the level of the problems they are trying to resolve. Personal life, knowledge, and history advance only obliquely. They do not go straight, without hesitation, toward goals or concepts. That which one too deliberately seeks, one does not achieve. On the contrary, ideas and values are a bounty to one who has learned to tap their source—in other words, to understand what he lives. At first they yield to our signifying and speaking life only like points of resistance in a diffused milieu, are circumscribed, the way perceived things are, only through the complicity of a background, presupposing as much shadow as light. We should not even say in this case that the ends prescribe the means. Ends are nothing but their common style, the total meaning of everyday means, the momentary shape of everyday meaning. And even the purest of truths presuppose marginal views. Not being entirely in the center of clear vision, they owe their meaning to the horizon which sedimentation and language preserve around them.

Here the reader may complain that we leave him empty and that we confine ourselves to "how things are," explaining nothing. But the fact is that explication consists in making clear what was obscure, juxtaposing what was implied. The proper place of explication is therefore at the beginning of our knowledge of nature—which is precisely when this knowledge believes it is dealing with a pure Nature. However, when it is a matter of speech or of the body or of history, where there is a risk of destroying what one is trying to understand, for example, of reducing language to thought or thought to language, one can only make visible the paradox of expression. Philosophy is the inventory of this dimension, which really speaking is universal, and a sphere where principles and consequences, ends and means, turn full circle. With respect to language, philosophy can only point out how, by the "coherent deformation" of gestures and sounds, man manages to speak an anonymous language and, through the "coherent deformation" of this language, to express what existed only for him.

4 / The Algorithm and the Mystery of Language

On several occasions, we have questioned the view that language is tied to what it signifies only by habit and convention. The relation is much closer and much more distant. In a sense, language turns its back on signification, and does not give it a thought. It is far less a table of statements which satisfy well-formed thoughts than a swarm of gestures all occupied with differentiating themselves from one another and blending again. The phonologists have well observed this sublinguistic life whose whole effort is to differentiate signs and systematize them. This observation is true not only of the phonemes prior to words but also of words and all of language, which is not first of all the sign of certain significations but the rule-governed power of differentiating the verbal chain according to the characteristic dimensions of each language. In a sense, language never has anything to do with anything but itself. In the internal monologue, as in the dialogue, there are no "thoughts." It is words that words arouse and, to the degree that we "think" more fully, words so precisely fill our minds that they leave no empty corner for pure thoughts or for significations that are not the work of language. The mystery is that, in the very moment where language is thus obsessed with itself, it is enabled, through a kind of excess, to open us to a signification. One could say that it is a law of the spirit to find only that for which the spirit has looked. In an instant this flow of words annuls itself as noise, throwing us completely into what it means. If we still reply to it with words, it is without wanting to. We no more think of the *words* that we are saying or that are being said to us than of the very hand we are shaking. The hand is not a bundle of flesh and bone, it is the palpable presence of the other person. Language has, therefore, a peculiar signification which is the more evident the more we surrender ourselves to it, and the less equivocal the less we think of it. This signification resists any direct seizure but is docile to the incantation of language. It is always there when one starts to evoke it but always a bit beyond the point where we think we discern it. As Paulhan says perfectly, the signification of language consists in "rays sensible to him who sees them but hidden from him who watches them," while language is made of "gestures which are not accomplished without some negligence." [1] Paulhan is the first to have seen that in use speech is not content with designating thoughts the way a street number designates my friend Paul's house. Speech in use really undergoes "a metamorphosis through which words cease to be accessible to our senses and lose their weight, their noise, their lines, their space (to become thoughts). But on its side thought renounces (to become words) its rapidity or its slowness, its surprise, its invisibility, its time, the internal consciousness that we have of it." [2] This, indeed, is the mystery of language.

But does not the mystery condemn us to silence? If language is comparable to that point in the eye of which physiologists speak as what helps us to see everything, according to the evidence it cannot see itself and cannot be observed. If language hides from anyone who seeks it and surrenders to anyone who renounces it, then one cannot look it in the face. One can only "think of it obliquely," "mime," or "reveal" its mystery.[3] All that remains is to "be" language, to which Paulhan seems to resign himself. Yet that is not possible precisely because of his own principles. One can no longer simply *be* language after one has questioned it. One would be returning to language knowingly and, as Paulhan has

1. Jean Paulhan, *Les Fleurs de Tarbes* (Paris: Gallimard, 1941), p. 177.

2. Jean Paulhan, *Clef de la poésie*, 2d ed. (Paris: Gallimard, 1944), p. 86.

3. *Ibid.*, p. 11.

said, it does not permit these measured obeisances. At the point of reflection reached by Paulhan, he could find the innocent use of language only in a second degree of language and *by speaking about it,* which is what we call philosophy. Even if we were only to "mime" or to "reveal" language, we would speak about language, and since what we would speak *about* would not be the same as we *who* speak about it, what we would say about it would be inadequate. The moment that we believe we are grasping the world as it is apart from us, it is no longer the world we are grasping, since we are there to grasp it. In the same way, there always remains, behind our talk about language, more living language than can ever be taken in by our view of it.

However, the situation is a dead end, the regressive movement in vain and philosophy in vain with it, only so long as it is a matter of explaining language, decomposing it, deducing it, grounding it, or operating in any other way to try to derive the clarity which belongs to a strange source. In this case, reflection, by virtue of being reflection and therefore speech, would always adopt whatever theme it chose and would in principle be incapable of achieving what it is seeking. But there are a philosophy and a mode of reflection which do not pretend to constitute their object, to be in rivalry with it, or to clarify it with a light that is not their own. People speak to me and I understand. When I have the feeling of dealing only with *words,* it is because expression has failed. When expression is successful, it seems to me that my thought is yonder, at the top of its voice, in those words that I have not spoken. Nothing is more convincing than this experience, and there is no need to look anywhere else than in it itself for what makes it evident, no need to replace the work of speech by some pure operation of spirit. All that is needed—and this is the whole of philosophy—is to cash in on this evidence, to confront it with the ready-made ideas we have of language and of the plurality of spirits. We need only reinstate this experience in its dignity as evidence, which it lost through the very use of language and because communication seems to us unproblematic. We need, finally, to restore what is paradoxical and even mysterious in this evidence, by providing it with an appropriate ground, from which it should be able to detach itself. We must conquer it as evidence, which is not just to use it, but quite the contrary. . . .

The best means of preserving the prodigious meaning we have found in language is not to silence it, to renounce philosophy, and to return to the immediate practice of language. Then the mystery would perish through familiarity. Language remains an enigma only to those who continue to question it, that is, to speak about it. Paulhan himself sometimes gets caught in this trap. He speaks of a "projection" of the self into the other, or of the other into me, which is the result of language.[4] But this implies a good deal of philosophy. The little word "projection" involves us in a theory of the relation between meaning and words. We may try to understand it as an analogous reasoning which would lead me to rediscover *my* thoughts in the other's words. But that is only pushing the problem farther back, since I am capable of understanding what I have never expressed. Thus we must have another idea of projection, according to which the other's speech not only awakes in me ready-made thoughts but also involves me in a movement of thought of which I would have been incapable alone and finally opens me to unfamiliar significations. Here, then, I would have to admit that I do not live just my own thought but that, in the exercise of speech, I *become* the one to whom I am listening. Finally, I would need to understand how speech can be pregnant with a meaning. Let us try, then, not to explain this but to establish more precisely the power of speaking, to get close to that signification which is nothing else than the unique movement of which signs are the visible trace.

Perhaps we shall see it better if we manage to rediscover it even in the cases where language restricts itself to saying nothing more than what has been decisively and precisely defined, to designating nothing but what language has already possessed. In other words, let us look where language denies its own past in order to reconstruct itself as an algorithm in which *in principle* the truth is no longer that floating spirit, ubiquitous but never with any location, which dwells in the language of literature and philosophy. There truth is instead an unmovable sphere of rela-

4. *Les Fleurs de Tarbes*, pp. 115 ff.

tions which were no less true prior to our formulations and would remain so even if all men and their language happened to disappear. As soon as integers appeared in human history, they announced themselves by certain properties which derive clearly from their definition. That is, if we find any new property in them, since it also derives from those which first served to delimit them, it appears equally old or contemporaneous with the integers themselves. Finally, if any still unknown property is revealed in the future, it seems that it already *belongs* to the integer. Even when it was not yet known that the sum of the n first integers is equal to the product of $\frac{n}{2}$ by $n + 1$, surely this relation existed between them? If it was an accident that led to the multiplication of $\frac{n}{2}$ by $n + 1$, would not a result equal to the sum of the n first integers have been found? Would not this coincidence have resulted here and now from the very structure of the series which would subsequently have grounded it? I had not yet noticed [5] that the series of the ten first integers is composed of five pairs of numbers whose sum is constant and equal to $10 + 1$. I had not yet understood that even this is demanded by the nature of the series, where the increase from 1 to 5 obeys exactly the same rhythm as the decrease from 10 to 6. But finally, even before I had recognized these relations, 10 increased by a unit was equal to 9 increased by 2, to 8 by 3, to 7 by 4, to 6 by 5, and the sum of these sums to that of the first ten integers. It seems that the changes of aspect which I introduced into the series by considering it from this new angle were contained in advance in the numbers themselves. When I *express* the relations unperceived until then, I limit myself to deducing them from a reservoir of truths which is the intelligible world of numbers.

When I introduce a new line into a drawing that changes its signification—for example, which results in the metamorphosis of a cube, seen in perspective, into a kitchen tile—there is no longer the same object before me. When the chimpanzee, wanting

5. The example is given and analyzed in these terms by Max Wertheimer, *Productive Thinking* (New York and London: Harper, 1945).

to get something beyond his reach, picks up a branch of a tree to use as a stick or borrows a stool to use as a ladder, his conduct shows that the branch in its new function is no longer a branch for him, that the stool ceases definitely to be a seat and becomes a ladder. The transformation is irreversible, and now it is not the *same* object which is treated each time from two perspectives. It is a branch which becomes a stick, it is a stool which becomes a ladder, the way a shake of a kaleidoscope makes a new pattern appear without my being able to recognize the old one in it. Between perceptual structures or structures of practical intelligence and the constructs of knowledge which open onto truth, there is a difference. The former, even when they resolve a problem and respond to a question of desire, recognize only blindly what they themselves contributed to the result. The latter arise from the *I can,* whereas the truth rises from an *I think,* from an inner recognition which traverses the length of the series of cognitive events, grounds its value, and posits it as an exemplar that is repeatable in principle by any consciousness placed in the same cognitive situation.

But if truth, to remain truth, presupposes this consorting of the self with itself, this inner unity through time, then the expressive operation which derives from Σn the formula $\frac{n}{2}(n+1)$ should be guaranteed by the immanence of the new in the ancient. It is not enough that the mathematician treats given relations according to certain formulae to transform them into the meaning of found relationships, the way the chimpanzee treats the branch of the tree in terms of what is useful to him to achieve his end. If the operation is to escape the contingency of the event and reveal a truth, it must itself be legitimated by the mathematical being on which it works. It seems, therefore, that one cannot give an account of exact knowledge except on condition of admitting, at least in this domain, a thought which abolishes all distance between the self and itself, which envelopes the expressive operation of its sovereign clarity, and reabsorbs in the algorithm the congenital obscurity of language. Here, at least, signification ceases to have that ambiguous relation to signs about which we have spoken. In language signification is fused with the juncture of signs; it is simultaneously tied to their bodily composition and blossoms mysteriously behind them. Signification bursts out above the signs and yet it is only their vibration, the way a cry carries outside and makes present to everyone the very breathing and pain of the man crying out. In the purity of the algorithm, signification is disengaged from all interference with the unfolding of signs which it rules and legitimates. By the same token, the signs correspond to the algorithm so exactly that the expression leaves nothing wanting and appears to us to contain meaning its very self. The jumbled relations of transcendence give way to the clear relations of a system of signs which have no inner life and a system of significations which do not descend into animal existence.

It is not our intention to question the character of *truth* which distinguishes the propositions of exact science or the incomparability of the moment where, in recognizing a truth, I touch on something that did not begin with me and will not cease to signify after me. This experience of an event which suddenly becomes hollow, losing its opacity, revealing a transparence, and becoming forever a meaning is a constant in culture and speech. If one wished to challenge the experience, he would not even know any more what he was seeking. All that can be done is to discover its implications, in particular whether, in relation to speech, it is originary or derivative. More precisely, one can discover whether, even in exact science, there exists, between the institutionalized signs and the *true* significations they designate, an instituting speech which is the vehicle of everything. When we say that the newly discovered properties of a mathematical entity are as old as it is, these very terms, "property" and "entity," already contain a whole interpretation of our experience of truth. Strictly, all we see is that certain supposedly given relations necessarily entail other relations. It is because we chose the first as principles and definitions that the others appear to us as *their* consequences. All we are entitled to say is that there is a solidarity of principle between them; that there are unbreakable ties such that, if certain relations are presupposed, so are others; that such and such relations are synonymous. This, of course, creates between given relations a relation of equivalence independent of its manifestation. This equivalence allows us to say that these relations constitute a system unaffected by time. But the new relations can have no other sense of existence than the relations from which they derive, and we never know whether these *are* anything more than mathematical entities—in other words, pure relations which we enjoy contemplating.

Henceforth we know that, although we are free to inquire into different objects (for example, different spaces), once an object is sufficiently determined we are no longer free to say anything whatsoever about it. This is, of course, a necessity which our mind encounters. However, the form in which it appears to us depends upon the starting point we have chosen. A proof is not a case of a certain mathematical entity imposing upon us properties which are its own. It is simply that there has to be a starting point and, once it has been determined, our freedom ends there, meeting its limit in the chain of consequences. Nothing reveals that the various forms that this limit to our freedom can take derive from the operation of an essence developing its own properties. Instead of saying that we establish certain *properties* of mathematical *entities*, we would be more exact if we said that we establish the possibility of the principle of enriching and making more precise the relations that served to define our object, of pursuing the construction of coherent mathematical wholes which our definitions merely outlined. To be sure, this possibility is not an empty thing, this coherence is not accidental, this validity is not illusory. But we cannot say that the new relations were true *before* they were revealed or that the first set of relations bring the later ones into existence. One could say so only if one were to hypothesize the first relations in some physical reality; the circle found in the sand already *had* equal radii, the triangle a sum of angles equal to two right angles . . . and all the other properties deducible by geometry. If we could subtract, from our conception of mathematical entities, any substratum of this kind, we would perceive it not as timeless but more as a development of knowledge.

This development is not fortuitous. Each of the advances that I stake out is *legitimate*. It is not just any old event; it is prescribed, and it is in any case justified afterward by the preceding steps. If essence is not the principle of our science, it is nevertheless present in our science as its goal. The development of knowledge moves toward the totality of a meaning. That is true. But essence conceived as the future of knowledge is not an essence; it is what we call a structure. Its relation to effective knowledge is like the relation of the thing perceived to perception. Perception, which is an event, opens onto the thing perceived, which appeared to be prior to perception and to be true before it. And if perception always reaffirms the preexistence of the world, it is precisely *because it* is an event, because the subject who perceives is already at grips with being through the *perceptual fields*, the "senses." More generally, the subject of perception is a body made to explore the world. Whatever stimulates the perceiving apparatus awakes a primordial familiarity between it and the world that we express by saying that the perceived existed before perception. In a single stroke, the immediate data of perception signify well beyond their own content, finding an inordinate echo in the perceiving subject. This is what enables the data to appear to us as perspectives upon a present object, whereas the explication of this object would proceed to infinity and would never be completed. Mathematical truth, reduced to what we truly establish, is not of a different kind. If we are almost irresistibly tempted, in conceiving the essence of the circle, to imagine a circle traced in the sand which already *has* all *its properties*, it is because our very notion of essence is formed in contact with an imitation of the perceived object as it is presented to us in perception, namely, as more ancient than perception itself, a self-contained, pure being prior to the subject. And since, as regards perception, it is not contradictory but rather its very definition *to be* an event and to *open on* a truth, we must also understand that truth in the service of mathematics is available to a subject already immersed in it and benefits from the carnal ties which unite them both.

We are not reducing mathematical evidence to perceptual evidence. We are certainly not denying, as will be seen, the originality of the order of knowledge vis-à-vis the perceptual order. We are trying only to loose the intentional web which ties them to one another, to rediscover the paths of the sublimation which preserves and transforms the perceived world into the spoken world. But this is possible only if we describe the operation of speech as a repetition, a reconquest of the world-thesis, analogous in its order to perception and yet different from it. The fact is that every mathematical idea presents itself to us with the character of a construction after the fact, a reconquest. Cultural constructions never have the solidity of natural objects. They are never there in the same way. Each morning, after night has intervened, we must make contact with them again. They remain impalpable; they float in the air of the village but the countryside does contain them. If, nevertheless, in the fullness of thought, the truths of culture seem to us the measure of being, and if so many philosophies posit the world upon them, it is because knowledge continues upon the thrust of perception. It is because knowledge uses the world-thesis which is its fundamental sound. We believe truth is eternal because truth expresses the perceived world and perception implies a world which was functioning before it and according to principles which it discovers and does not posit. In one and the same movement knowledge roots itself in perception and distinguishes itself from perception. Knowledge is an effort to recapture, to internalize, truly to possess a meaning that escapes perception at the very moment that it takes shape there, because it is interested only in the echo that being draws from itself, not in this resonator, its own other which makes the echo possible. Perception opens us to a world already constituted and can only reconstitute it. This reduplication signifies both that the world offers itself as prior to perception and that we do not limit ourselves to registering the world but would like to engender it. The meaning of the perceived object already is the shadow cast by the operations we bring to bear upon things. It is nothing other than our viewpoint on them, our situation with respect to them. Each vector of the perceived spectacle posits, beyond its aspect at the moment, the principle of certain equivalences in the possible variations of the spectacle. It inaugurates on its own account a *style* of the explication of objects and a *style* of our movements with respect to them. This mute or operational language of perception begins a process of knowledge which it cannot itself accomplish. However firm my perceptive grasp of the world may be, it is entirely dependent upon a centrifugal movement which throws me toward the world. I can recapture my grasp only if I myself spontaneously posit new dimensions of its signification. Here is the beginning of speech, the style of knowledge, truth in the logician's sense. It is called forth from its first movement by perceptual evidence which it continues without being reducible to perceptual evidence.

Once there is a clear reference to the world-thesis—which is always *understood* by mathematical thought and is what enables mathematical thought to present itself as the reflection of an intelligible world—how are we to understand mathematical truth? Above all—that is our aim—how are we to understand the algorithmic expression yielded by mathematical thought? It is clear, first of all, that the "properties" of the series of integers are not "contained" in that series. Once the series is clear of the perceptual analogy which makes "something" (*etwas überhaupt*) of the mathematical expression, it is at each moment nothing but the ensemble of relations established within it *plus an open horizon of relations that can be constructed.* This horizon is not the mode of presentation of a self-contained mathematical entity; at every moment, there is really nothing in heaven or on earth but the known properties of the integer. One may say, if one wishes, that the unknown properties are already operative in the ensemble of objects which embody the numbers. But that is only a manner of speaking. One is trying to express by it that everything that will be revealed about numbers will also be true of numbered objects, which is quite certain but does not entail any preexistence of the truth.

The new relation, $\frac{n}{2}(n + 1)$, this new signification of the series of integers, appears in it only if one reconsiders and restructures Σn. I must notice that the progression from 1 to 5 is exactly symmetrical with the regression from 10 to 5, so that I can then conceive a constant value of the sums $10 + 1$, $9 + 2$, $8 + 3$, etc., and, finally, so that I can decompose the series into pairs each equal to $n + 1$, whose total can only be equal to $\frac{n}{2}$. Of course, these transformations, which are the equivalent in the arithmetical object of a geometric construction, are always possible. I assure myself that they do not hold by some accident but derive from the structure which defines the series of numbers—and in this sense they are its result. But *they are not a part of it;* they emerge only when I address a certain question to the *structure* of the series of numbers, or rather when the structure poses a question to me insofar as it is an open and incomplete situation, as it offers itself as something *to be known.* The operation through which I express Σn in the terms $\frac{n}{2}(n + 1)$ is possible only if I perceive in the last formula the double function of n, first as a cardinal number, then as an ordinal number. It is not by any blind transformation that I am then able to pass to $\frac{n+1}{2}n$, or to $\frac{n(n+1)}{2}$, or to $\frac{n^2+n}{2}$. I see that $\frac{n}{2}(n + 1)$ results from Σn by virtue of the structure of Σn. Then I understand what is involved in a mathematical truth. And, even if I proceed to exploit the formula I obtain by mechanical counting procedures, it is then only a question of a secondary and minor operation which teaches us nothing about what truth is.

Nothing in what we are saying would be changed if it were possible to constitute an algorithm which expressed the logical properties of the series of whole numbers. The moment these formal relations yielded—and this is the hypothesis—an exact equivalent of the structure of number, they, like the latter, would provide the occasion for the construction of a new relation rather than containing it. We are trying to show not that mathematical thought rests upon the sensible but that it is creative. Creativity could also be shown for a formalized mathematics. Since the results are achieved through deduction and apply only to the definition of the integer, once I have arrived at the result I can as well say that the formula I obtain is derived strictly from the initial definitions or that the series itself determines its new significance. That is how my present knowledge views its own past; that is not how it happened, even behind the scene. The results were not immanent in the hypothesis. They were prefigured in the structure only as an open system and were caught in the development of my thought. When I vary this structure in terms of its own vectors, it is rather the new configuration which repeats and preserves the old one, contains it eminently, identifying with it, or recognizing it as indistinguishable from itself. The synthesis is the result of the development of my knowledge and not its precondition. Non-Euclidean geometries contain Euclid's geometry as a particular case but not the inverse. What is essential to mathematical thought, therefore, lies in the moment where a structure is decentered, opens up to questioning, and reorganizes itself according to a new meaning which is nevertheless the meaning of this same structure. The truth of the result, its value independent of the content, consists in its not involving a *change* in which the initial relations dissolve, to be replaced by others in which they would be unrecognizable. Rather, the truth lies in a restructuring which, from one end to the other, is known to itself, is congruent with itself, a restructuring which was announced in the vectors of the initial structure by its style, so that each effective change is the fulfillment of an intention, and each anticipation receives from the structure the completion it needed.

We are dealing here with a veritable *development of meaning*. The *development* is not an objective succession, a transformation of fact, but a self-development, a development of meaning. When I say that there is truth here, I do not mean that, between the hypothesis and the conclusion, I experience a relation of identity that leaves nothing wanting or that I see the one's deriving from the other in an absolute transparence. There is no signification which is not surrounded by an horizon of naïve beliefs and is thus not in need of other clarifications. There is no expressive operation that exhausts its object. Euclid's demonstrations were rigorous, although they were always encumbered with a coefficient of facticity that rested upon a massive intuition of space which could be made thematic only later. In order for there to be truth, the restructuring which yields a new meaning must truly repeat the initial structure, even though it has its gaps and opacities. New thematizations subsequently will fill the gaps and dissolve the opacities but, apart from the fact that they themselves will be partial, they will not make a Euclidean triangle, for example, have properties other than those we know it has. The legitimate transformations which lead from the Euclidean universe to its properties will remain something that can be understood and needs only to be translated into a more general language. The proper domain of truth is therefore this repetition of the object of thought in its new signification, even if the object still retains in its crevices relations that we use without being aware of them. The fact is that at this moment something is acquired, there is a step toward truth, the structure propels itself toward its transformations.

The awareness of truth advances like a crab, turned toward its point of departure, toward that structure *whose* signification it expresses. Such is the living operation that sustains the signs of the algorithm. If one considered the result alone, one could believe that nothing has been created. In the formula $\frac{n}{2}(n + 1)$, only terms borrowed from the hypothesis, related through algebraic operations, enter. The new signification is represented by the initial signs and significations, and they are deflected from their original meaning, as happens in language. The algorithmic expression is *exact* because of the exact equivalence established between its initial relations and those that are derived from them. But the new formula is only a formula *of* the new signification and expresses it truly only if, for example, we gave to the term n first its ordinal meaning and then its cardinal meaning. This is possible only if we refer to the configuration of the series of numbers under the new aspect which our interrogation brings to it. But here there reappears the *shift* of restructuring which is characteristic of language. Once we have managed to find the formula, we then forget the shift, and so we believe in the preexistence of the world. But the shift is still there and it alone gives meaning to the formula. The algorithmic expression is therefore secondary. It is a special case of language. We believe that in this case signs repeat the intention exactly, that the signification is captured without remainder, and finally that the style which prescribed the structural transformations that we introduced is entirely ruled by us. But that is because we omitted mention of the structure's transcendence toward its transformations. To be sure, this transcendence is always possible in principle, since we consider only the invariants in our study of structure and not the accidental peculiarities of a line or a figure. But we are dealing with a transcendence and not a static identity, and here, as in language, truth is not an adequation but anticipation, repetition, and slippage of meaning. Truth allows itself to be reached only through a sort of distance. The thing thought is not the thing perceived. Knowledge is not perception, speech is not one gesture among all the other gestures. For speech is the vehicle of our movement toward truth, as the body is the vehicle of our being in the world.

5 / Dialogue and the Perception of the Other

IN THE ALGORITHM and exact science we speak about *things*. Nothing is presupposed upon the part of the ideal interlocutor but a knowledge of definitions. There is no attempt to seduce him and no expectation of complicity on his part. In principle, the algorithm and exact science lead him, as it were by the hand, from what he knows to what he ought to learn, without his having to abandon internal evidence for the drift of language. But if even in this realm of pure significations and pure signs, new meaning emerges from the old only through a transformation which is made outside of the algorithm and is always presupposed by it, and if mathematical truth appears only to a subject for whom there are structures, situations, and a perspective—with all the more reason should we admit that "languaged" [*langagière*] knowledge arouses transformations in the given significations which were contained in it only in the way French literature is contained in the French language or a writer's future works in his style. Similarly, we should define the very function of speech as its power to say as a whole more than it says word by word, to precede itself, whether in throwing the other toward what I know which he has not yet understood, or in carrying oneself toward what one is going to understand.

It is speech which accomplishes those anticipations, encroachments, transgressions, those violent operations through which I build within the form and change its operation to make literature and philosophy turn into what they are, to change them into themselves. To be sure, the physical fact of a new line does not represent a geometric construction. And in the arts of speech, the physical existence of sounds, the traces of the words on paper, or even the actual presence of such words according to their dictionary sense or stock phrases in no way suffices to yield a meaning. The operation of meaning has its own internal side of which the whole flow of words is only a wake, an indication of only its cross-points. But established significations contain the new signification only as a trace or a horizon. The new signification will later recognize itself in them, but even when it takes them up again it will forget what was partial and naïve in them. The new signification only relights sudden flashes in the depths of past knowledge, touching past knowledge only from a distance. From the past knowledge to the new signification there is an invocation, and from the new signification in turn there are a response to and acquiescence in past knowledge.

The flow of words from which a book is made is bound together by an almost imperceptible inflection of ordinary usage, the consistency of a certain eccentricity. On entering a room, one can see that *something* has been changed, without being able to say what. On picking up a book, I find that all the words have changed, without being able to say into what. As an innovation of usage, defined by a certain and consistent deviation which we are unable to explain at first, the meaning of a book is lingual.

The configurations of our world are all altered because one of them has been torn from its simple existence in order to represent all the others and to become the key or style of this world, a general means of interpreting it. We often hear of those Cartesian "ideas" which are scattered in St. Augustine and even Aristotle. However, there they had only a dull life without any future, as if the whole signification of an idea were dependent upon its prominence, its associations, for clarification. St. Augustine came upon the *cogito*, Descartes upon occasionalism in the *Dioptics;* Balzac once caught the tone of Giradoux—but they all failed to realize that they had made these anticipations, and Descartes still has to do his part after St. Augustine, Giradoux after Balzac. Thus the highest point of truth is still only perspective.

We affirm, alongside the analytic truth espoused by the algorithm and leaving aside the possibility of the algorithm's being detached from the thinking life in which it is born, a truth of transparency, recovery, and recollection, in which we participate, not insofar as we think *the same thing* but insofar as we are, each in his own way, moved and touched by it. The writer too speaks of the world and of things, he does not pretend to speak in the general name. He speaks to his audience according to the way that its members have of abiding in the world, of confronting life and death. He takes them just where they are and, by working with objects, events, men, intervals, plans, and openings, he touches in them their most secret foundations, getting at their fundamental ties with the world and thus transforms their deepest partiality into a means of truth. The algorithm speaks about things and in addition reaches men. Writing speaks to men and rejoins truth through them. We shall completely understand this trespass of things upon their meaning, this discontinuity of knowledge which is at its highest point in speech, only when we understand it as the trespass of oneself upon the other and of the other upon me. . . .

Let us pursue dialogue a little further—and first of all, in the silent relationship with the other—if we wish to understand the most essential power of speech.

It is not sufficiently noted that the other is never present face to face. Even when, in the heat of discussion, I directly confront my adversary, it is not in that violent face with its grimace, or even in that voice traveling toward me, that the intention which reaches me is to be found. The adversary is never quite localized; his voice, his gesticulations, his twitches, are only effects, a sort of stage effect, a ceremony. Their producer is so well masked that I am quite surprised when my own responses carry over. This marvelous megaphone becomes embarrassed, gives a few sighs, a few tremors, some *signs of intelligence*. One must believe that there was someone over there. But where? Not in that overstrained voice, not in that face lined like any well-worn object. Certainly not *behind* that setup: I know quite well that back there there is only "darkness crammed with organs." The other's body is in front of me—but as far as it is concerned, it leads a singular existence, *between* I who think and that body, or rather near me, by my side. The other's body is a kind of replica of myself, a wandering double which haunts my surroundings more than it appears in them. The other's body is the unexpected response I get from elsewhere, as if by a miracle things began to tell my thoughts, or as though they would be thinking and speaking always for me, since they are things and I am myself.[1] The other, in my eyes, is thus always on the margin of what I see and hear, he is this side of me, he is beside or behind me, but he is not in that place which my look flattens and empties of any "interior." Every other is a self like myself. He is like that double which the sick man feels always at his side, who resembles him like a brother, upon whom he could never fix without making him disappear, and who is visibly only the outside prolongation of himself, since a little attention suffices to extinguish him. Myself and the other are like two *nearly* concentric circles which can be distinguished only by a slight and mysterious slippage. This alliance is perhaps what will enable us to understand the relation to the other that is inconceivable if I try to approach him directly, like a sheer cliff.

Nevertheless, the other is not I and on that account differences must arise. I make the other in my own image, but how *can there be for me an image of myself*? Am I not to the very end of the universe, am I not, by myself, coextensive with everything I can see, hear, understand, or feign? How could there be an outside view upon this totality which I am? From where could it be had? Yet that is just what happens when the other appears to me. To the infinity that was me something else still adds itself; a sprout shoots forth, I grow; I give birth, this other is made from my flesh and blood and yet is no longer me. How is that possible? How can the *cogito* emigrate beyond me, since it is me? The looks with which I scan the world, like a blind man tapping objects with his cane, are seized by someone at the other

1. EDITOR: The text of this sentence is clearly unfinished. After "tell my thoughts," Merleau-Ponty began two subordinate clauses which he crossed out. On rereading, he undoubtedly added "as though" which he left unconnected. TRANSLATOR: I have adapted the English to suit this observation.

end and sent back to touch me in turn. It is no longer enough for me to feel: I feel that someone feels me, that he feels both my feeling and my feeling the very fact that he feels me. . . . It is not enough simply to say that henceforth I inhabit another body. That would only make a second me, a second dwelling for me. But *there is a myself which is other,* which dwells elsewhere and deprives me of my central location, although, from all the evidence, he can acquire his quality of self only through filiation. The roles of the subject and of what he sees are exchanged and reversed. I thought I gave to what I see its meaning as a thing seen, and then one of these things suddenly slips out of this condition. The spectacle begins to furnish itself a spectator who is not I but who is reproduced from me. How is that possible? How can I see something that begins to see?

As we have said, we shall never understand how it is that another can appear to us; what is before us is an object. We must understand that the problem does not lie there but is to understand how I can make myself into two, how I can decenter myself. The experience of the other is always that of a replica of myself, of a response to myself. The solution must be sought in the direction of that strange filiation which makes the other forever my second, even when I prefer him to myself and sacrifice myself to him. It is in the very depths of myself that this strange articulation with the other is fashioned. The mystery of the other is nothing but the mystery of myself. A second spectator upon the world can be born from me. I make this possible myself if I take account at all of my own paradoxes. That which makes me unique, my fundamental capacity for *self*-feeling, tends paradoxically to diffuse itself. It is because I am a totality that I am capable of giving birth to another and of seeing myself limited by him. For the miracle of the perception of another lies first of all in that everything which qualifies as a being to my eyes does so only by coming, whether directly or not, within my range, by reckoning in my experience, entering my world. This means that everything which is true is mine and everything which is mine is true and claims for its witness not only myself within my limits but still another X, and at the limit an absolute spectator —supposing another or an absolute spectator were conceivable.

Everything is ready in me to receive these testimonies. We must learn how they could ever be introduced so as to get to me, all the more because my own evidence is mine and my field holds for me as the universal locus of being.

I am watching this man who is motionless in sleep and suddenly he wakes. He opens his eyes. He makes a move toward his hat, which has fallen beside him, and picks it up to protect himself from the sun. What finally convinces me that my sun is the same as his, that he sees and feels it as I do, and that after all there are two of us perceiving the world, is precisely that which, at first, prevented me from conceiving the other—namely, that his body belongs among my objects, that it is one of them, that it appears in my world. When the man asleep in the midst of my objects begins to make gestures toward them, to make use of them, I cannot doubt for a moment that the world to which he is oriented is truly the same world that I perceive. *If he perceives something,* that something must be my own world, since it is there that he comes into being. But why should he perceive it, how am I able even to conceive that he may do so? If what he is going to see inevitably is the very same as what is perceived by me, at least his own perception of the world which I am just supposing has no place in my world. Where would I put it? It is not in that body, which is nothing but tissue, blood, and bone. It is not in the trajectory from that body to the things, because in that trajectory there are only more things, or luminous beams, vibrations, and it is now ages since we abandoned the images of Epicurus. As for the "spirit," that is I and so I cannot put into it that other perception of the world. Thus the other is not to be found in the things, he is not in his body, and he is not I. We cannot put him anywhere and effectively we put him nowhere, neither in the in-itself nor in the for-itself, which is me. There is no place for him except in *my field,* but that place at least was ready for him ever since I began to perceive. From the first time I relied on my body to explore the world, I knew that this corporeal relation to the world could be generalized. A shifting distance was established between me and the being which reserved the rights of another perception of the same being. The other is nowhere in being. He slips into my perception from behind. The experience that I make out of my hold on the world is what makes me capable of perceiving another myself, provided that in the interior of my world there opens up a gesture resembling my own. The moment the man wakes up in the sun and reaches for his hat, between the sun which burns *me* and makes *my* eyes squint and the gesture which from a distance *over there* brings relief to my fatigue, between this sweating forehead and the protective gesture which it calls forth on my part, a bond is tied without my needing to decide anything. If I am forever incapable of effectively living the experience of the scorching the other suffers, the bite of the world as I feel it upon my body is an injury for anyone exposed to it as I am—and especially for this body which begins to defend itself against it. It is this bite which starts to stir the sleeper previously motionless who now begins to adjust to his gestures as their reason for being.

As long as it adheres to my body like the tunic of Nessus, the world exists not only for me but for everyone in it who makes gestures toward it. There is a universality of feeling—and it is upon this that our identification rests, the generalization of my body, the perception of the other. I perceive behavior immersed in the same world as I because the world I perceive still trails with it my corporeality. My perception is the impact of the world upon me and the catch of my gestures toward it—which is such that, between the things sought for by the sleeper's movements and the movements themselves, insofar as they each make up part of my field, there is not only the external relation of one object to another but, as though from the world to me, an impact, and from me to the world, a catch.

If I am still asked how I am brought to entrust to "others" my own role of the incarnate subject and just how the other's movements can appear to me as gestures, so that the automaton comes alive and the other is there, in the last analysis I must answer that it is because neither the body of the other nor the objects he regards have ever been pure objects for me. They are internal to my field and to my world, and thus they are altogether variations of that fundamental relation (even of things, I say that one "looks" toward the other or "turns his back" upon it). One field does not exclude another the way an act of absolute consciousness, a decision, for example, excludes another. Rather, a field tends of itself to multiply, because it is the opening through which, as a body, I am "exposed" to the world. Thus it does not have that absolute density of a pure consciousness which makes every other consciousness an impossibility for it—for, being itself generality, the field can hardly grasp itself other than as one of its likenesses. . . . This means that there would not be others or other minds for me, if I did not have a body and if they had no body through which they slip into my field, multiplying it from within, and seeming to me prey to the same world, oriented to the same world as I. That everything which exists for me should be mine, and not qualify as a being for me except on condition of being framed in my field, does not prevent the appearance of the other—on the contrary, it makes that appearance possible, because my relation to myself is already generality. It is because of this, as we said in the beginning, that the other always slips in at the junction between the world and ourselves, that he is always this side of things and rather on our side than in them. The other, then, is a generalized I. He has his place not in objective space, which, as Descartes has said, is without mind, but in that anthropological "locality," that ambiguous space where nonreflective perception moves at its ease, though always on the margin of reflection, impossible to constitute, always already constituted. We find the other the same way we find our body. As soon as we look him in the face, the other is reduced to the modest condition of something innocent that one can hold at a distance. Moreover, he exists in the back of us, just as things acquire their absolute independence on the margin of our visual field. There have often, and rightly, been protests against the expedient whereby psychologists seeking to explain how, for example, nature is animated for us, or how there are other minds, get around it by speaking about a "projection" of ourselves into things. But this evasion misses the question entirely, since we still want to know what it is about the very look of external objects which invites this our projection and how things are able to "signify" to mind. Here we are not thinking of the psychological concept of projection which makes our experience of ourselves or of the body spill over upon an external world with which it has in principle no relation. On the contrary, we are trying to awaken a carnal relation to the world and the other that is not an accident intruding from outside upon a pure cognitive subject (how would he receive it within him?) or a "content" of experience among many others but our first insertion into the world and into truth.

Perhaps now we are closer to understanding better the accomplishment language represents for us, how language prolongs and transforms the silent relation with the other. In a sense, the other's words do not pierce our silence. They are unable to give us anything more than his gestures. The same difficulty is involved in understanding how words arranged in propositions can signify anything else to us except our own thought, how the movements of a body patterned into gestures or actions can present us with someone else than ourselves, how we are able to find in these spectacles anything other than we have put into them. The solution is the same. It consists, as far as our silent relation to the other is concerned, in understanding that our sensibility to the world, our synchronized relations to it—that is, our body—the thesis underlying all our experiences removes from our existence the density of an absolute and unique act, making a transferable signification of our "corporeality," creating a "common situation," and finally yielding the perception of another like ourselves, if not in the absolute of his effective existence then at least in its general outline accessible to us. In the same way, with respect to the particular gesture of speech, the solution lies in recognizing that, in the experience of the dialogue, the other's speech manages to reach in us our significations, and that our words, as the replies attest, reach in him his significations. For we encroach upon one another inasmuch as we belong to the same cultural world, and above all to the same language, and my acts of expression and the other's derive from the same institution.

All the same, this "general" usage of speech presupposes another, more fundamental practice—just as my coexistence with my likenesses presupposes that I have first recognized them as likenesses—in other words, that my field should have shown itself an inexhaustible source of being—not only of being for me but also of being for the other. Just as our common membership in the same world presupposes that my experience, insofar as it is original, should be the experience of being, so our membership in a common language or even a common universe of language presupposes a primordial relation between me and my speech, which gives it the value of a dimension of being in which I can participate. Through this relation, the other myself can become other and can become myself in a much more radical sense. The common language which we speak is something like the anonymous corporeality which we share with other organisms. The simple use of this language, like the institutionalized conduct of which I am the agent and witness, yields another only in general, diffused through my field, an anthropological or cultural space, a species-individual, so to speak, and finally a notion rather than a presence. But the expressive operation, and speech in particular considered in its nascent state, establish a common situation which is no longer only a community of *being* but a community of *doing.** It is here that the enterprise of communication has really occurred and silence seems to be broken. Between the "natural" gesture (if we could ever find one that did not presuppose or create an entire structure of significations) and speech, the difference is that the natural gesture points out objects given to our senses from elsewhere, whereas the expressive gesture, in particular speech, is charged with revealing

* This arises because speech is not oriented to the natural world but to the world of spontaneity—not *sensible.* At this level, what becomes of the invisible other? He is still invisible, on my side, behind me, etc. But not insofar as we share the same prehistory: insofar as we share in the same *speech.* This speech is like the other in general, ungraspable, unthematizable, and, to that extent, it is generality, not individuality. But it is as though the individuality of feeling had been sublimated to the point of communication. It is this speech that we have in mind and which therefore does not rest on generality alone. It has to be more than objective, more than meaningful. There is in it no difference between single being and meaning. No opposition between my language and my work, between particular and universal. Here the other is grafted onto the same. Speaking and hearing are indiscernible. To speak to and to be spoken to. We continue. . . . But at the same time violence of speech. More-than-meaning. Sympathy of totalities.

relations not only between terms given from elsewhere but even the very terms of these relations.

The cultural sedimentation which bestows upon our words and gestures an accepted common background had itself to be built up from these very same words and gestures, and a little fatigue suffices to break this most basic communication. At this point in the explanation of communication, we cannot do more than invoke our membership in a common world. It is this membership which is involved here, and we must give an account of it. At best, we may say that our roots in the same land and our experience of the same nature are what launch us in the enterprise. They could not guarantee it, and they would not be sufficient to accomplish it.

The moment the first "human" signification has been expressed, an enterprise has been embarked upon which surpasses our common prehistory even though prolonging its movement. It is this conquering speech which interests us, for it makes institutionalized speech, or language, possible. Speech has to teach its own meaning to both the speaker and the listener. It is not enough for speech to convey a meaning already given to either side. Speech must bring meaning into existence. Thus it is essential for speech to transcend itself as gesture. Speech is the gesture which suppresses itself as such and goes beyond itself toward a meaning. Prior to all institutionalized language and their life support, speech is carried into existence by them. Once common significations have been institutionalized, speech's work carries over even further. It is therefore necessary to conceive the operation of speech as outside any previously institutionalized signification, as a unique act whereby a man's speaking furnishes his listener and a culture that is common to them. Certainly, speech is nowhere visible. Like the other, I cannot assign speech a location. Like the other, it is more this side of me than among things. But I cannot even say that speech may be "in me," since it is equally "in the listener." Speech is peculiarly my own, *my* productivity, and yet speech is so only to make meaning out of my productivity and to communicate that meaning. The other who listens and understands joins with me in what is most singular in me. It is as though the universality of feeling of which we have spoken has finally ceased to be a universality for me and in the end redoubled itself through a recognized universality. The other's words, or mine in him, do not limit themselves to vibrating like chords the listener's machinery of acquired significations or to arousing some reminiscence. Their flow must have the power of throwing me in turn toward a signification that neither he nor I possessed before. In watching an organism orient gestures toward its environment, I begin to perceive its perceiving because the internal organization of its gestures is the same as my own conduct and tells me of my own relation to the world—in the same way, when I speak to another person and listen to him, what I understand begins to insert itself in the intervals between my saying things, my speech is intersected laterally by the other's speech, and I hear myself in him, while he speaks in me. Here it is the same thing *to speak to* and *to be spoken to*. This is the irreducible fact that all militant speech harbors and which literary expression brings before us, if ever we were tempted to forget it.

Speech endlessly renews the mediation of the same and the other. Speech perpetually verifies for us that there is no signification without a movement, at first violent, that surpasses all signification. My relation to a book begins with the easy familiarity of the words of our language, of ideas that are part of our makeup, in the same way that my perception of the other is at first sight perception of the gestures and behavior belonging to "the human species." But if the book really teaches me something, if the other person is really another, at a certain stage I must be surprised, disoriented. If we are to meet not just through what we have in common but in what is different between us—which presupposes a transformation of myself and of the other as well—then our differences can no longer be opaque qualities. They must become meaning. In the perception of the other, this happens when the other organism, instead of "behaving" like me, engages with the things in my world in a style that is at first mysterious to me but which at least seems to me a coherent style because it responds to certain possibilities which fringed the things in my world. Similarly, when I am reading, there must be a certain moment where the author's intention escapes me, where he withdraws himself. Then I catch up from behind, fall into step, or else I turn over a few pages and, a bit later, a happy phrase brings me back and leads me to the core of the new signification, and I find access to it through one of its "aspects" which was already part of my experience.

Rationality, or the agreement of minds, does not require that we all reach the same idea by the same road, or that significations be enclosed in definitions. It requires only that every experience contain points of catch for all other ideas and that "ideas" have a configuration. This double requirement is the postulation of a *world.* However, it is not a question here of the unity attested by the universality of feeling, since the unity of which we are speaking is invoked rather than verified, and since it is *almost* invisible and constructed on the edifice of our signs. Thus we call this universality the "cultural world," and we call speech our power of making use of certain conveniently organized things—black and white, the sound of the voice, movements of the hand—to put in relief, to differentiate, to master, to treasure the significations which trail on the horizon of the sensible world, or even more to breathe into the opacity of the sensible that void which will make it transparent but which itself, like the air blown into a bottle, never lacks some substantial reality. Our perception of living others finally depends upon the evidence of the sensed world which is open to other and yet comprehensible ways of behaving. In the same way, the perception of a veritable alter ego presupposes that his talk, at the point where we understand him and especially at the moment he withdraws from us and threatens to fall into non-sense, be capable of remaking us in his image and to open us to another meaning. This is a power which he does not possess before me as mind: a mind can find in things only what it has put into them. He is able to get across to me inasmuch as I am also speech, that is, capable of allowing myself to be led by the flow of talk toward a new state of knowledge.

Between myself as speech and the other as speech, or more generally myself as expression and the other as expression, there is no longer that alternation which makes a rivalry of the relation between minds. I am not active only when speaking; rather,

I precede my thought in the listener. I am not passive while I am listening; rather, I speak according to . . . what the other is saying. Speaking is not just my own initiative, listening is not submitting to the initiatve of the other, because as speaking subjects we are *continuing,* we are resuming a common effort more ancient than we, upon which we are grafted to one another and which is the manifestation, the growth, of truth. We say that the true has always been true, but that is a confused way of saying that all preceding expressions revive and receive their place in the expression of the present, which makes it possible, if one wishes, to read the present in them after the fact but, more justly, to recover them in the present expression. The foundation of truth is not outside of time; it is in the opening of each moment of knowledge to those who will resume it and change its sense. What we call speech is nothing but such anticipation and repetition, this touching from a distance, which cannot be grasped in terms of contemplation. It is rather a profound connivance of time with itself. The living relation between speaking subjects is masked because one always adopts, as the model of speech, the *statement* or the *indicative.* One does so because one believes that, apart from statements, there remain only stammering and foolishness. Thus one overlooks how the tacit, unformulated, and nonthematized enters into science, contributing to the determination of science's meaning, and as such provide tomorrow's science with its field of investigation. One overlooks the whole of literary expression, where we must precisely mark out what may be called "oversignification" and distinguish it from non-sense.

In basing signification upon speech, we wish to say it is essential to signification never to appear except as the sequel to a discourse already under way. Signification seems to precede the writings in which it is manifest, not because they bring down to earth ideas that preexisted in an intelligible heaven or in the Nature of Things, but because it is the achievement of each word not only to be the expression of *this here* but also to surrender itself entirely as a fragment of universal discourse, to announce a system of interpretation. It is aphasiacs who, in order to carry on a conversation, need "resting points" chosen in advance or, in order to write on a blank page, need some indication—a line traced before they start or just a spot of ink on the paper—which pulls them back from the vertigo of the void and allows them to *begin*. But—if one can reproach excessive impulsiveness and the lack—it is Mallarmé, at the other extreme of the field of speech, who is fascinated by the empty page because he wanted to say everything. He postponed indefinitely writing The Book, leaving us in the name of his *works* writings which circumstances snatched from him—but which his weakness, his fortunate weakness, furtively allowed itself. The happy writer and the speaking man are neither so greatly nor so little conscientious. They do not wonder, before speaking, whether speech is possible. They do not contemplate the sorrow of language which is the necessity of not saying everything if one is to say something. They sit happily in the shade of a great tree and continue aloud the internal monologue. Their thought germinates in speech and, without seeking it, they are understood, making themselves other, while saying what is most singular to them. They truly abide in themselves, without feeling exiled from the other. And because they are fully convinced that what seems evident to them is true, they say it quite simply. They cross bridges of snow without seeing how fragile those are, using to the very limit that extraordinary power given to every mind of convincing others and entering into their little corner when it believes itself to be coextensive with the truth.

Everyone, in a sense, is the whole of the world to himself, and, by that grace, once he is convinced of this it becomes true. For then he speaks, others understand him—and the private totality fraternizes with the social whole. In speech we realize the impossible agreement between two rival totalities not because speech forces us back upon ourselves to discover some unique spirit in which we participate but because speech concerns us, catches us indirectly, seduces us, trails us along, transforms us into the other and him into us, abolishes the limit between mine and not-mine, and ends the alternative between what has sense for me and what is non-sense for me, between me as subject and the other as object. It is well that some people try to set up obstacles to the intrusion of this spontaneous power and oppose it with their rigor and ill will. But their silence ends in further words, and rightly so. There is no silence that is pure attention and that, having begun nobly, remains equal to itself. As Maurice Blanchot remarked, Rimbaud transcends speech and ends by *writing more*. But it is these letters from Abyssinia which, without a trace of humor, demand an honest competence, a family and public consideration. . . . Thus one always accepts the movement of expression; one does not cease to be tributary to expression by having rejected it. In the end, what should we call this power to which we are vowed, and which, however we feel, pulls significations from us? Certainly, it is not a god, since its operation depends upon us. It is not an evil genius, since it bears the truth. It is not the "human condition"—or, if it is "human," it is so in the sense that man destroys the generality of the species and brings himself to admit others into his deepest singularity. It is still by calling it speech or spontaneity that we best designate this ambiguous gesture which makes the universal out of singulars and meaning out of our life.

6 / Expression and the Child's Drawing

NOWADAYS WE ENCOURAGE every form of illusive and allusive expression, especially pictorial expression, and in particular the art of the "primitives," the drawings of children and madmen, as well as every genre of involuntary poetry, the "testament" or spoken language. But, with the exception of certain contemporary figures whose neurosis is their sole talent, the resort to brute expression has not occurred in opposition to the art of the museums or against classical literature. On the contrary, it is natural for us to keep these alive by recalling the creative power of expression which sustains "objective" art and literature as well as the other forms, though we no longer feel through them, precisely because we are settled, as though on natural ground, in the traditions they have left us. After the experience of noncanonical styles of expression, classical art and literature appear as the hitherto most successful mastery of an expressive power which is not grounded upon nature but reveals such eloquence in the classics that whole centuries have believed that the power was coextensive with the world.

For us, then, classical art and literature have become once again what they had never ceased to be: a historical creation—with all which that implies as to risk and also partiality or narrowness. What we call *significant* art and literature are significant only in a certain cultural area and must therefore be connected with a more general power of signification. Objective art and literature, which claim to appeal only to significations already present in every man and every thing, are in form and substance inventions. Objectivity exists only because, in the first place, a transobjective [*surobjectif*] power of expression opened up for centuries a common field of language. There is signification only because a transsignificant [*sursignifiant*] informed itself, made itself understood of itself, through the same risk and partiality as any creation. Before inquiring, in the following chapter,[1] into the nature of the relationships between the power of expression and the thinker whom it presupposes and shapes, as well as the history which it continues and re-creates, let us confront this expressive power directly with its contingency and its risks.

The objectivist illusion is firmly established in us. We are convinced that the expressive act in its normal or fundamental form consists, given a signification, in the construction of a system of signs such that, for each element of the signified, there corresponds a signifying element—in other words, in *representation*. From this postulate we begin the examination of the most elliptical expressions—which are by the same token discounted—for example, children's expression. In this case, given some object or spectacle, representation would consist in reporting it and making a sort of equivalent of it on paper in such a way that, in principle, every element of the spectacle is indicated unequivocally and without impingement. The two-dimensional perspective is clearly the only solution of the problem posed in these terms, and so the development of children's drawing is described as a progression toward perspective.

Earlier we showed that two-dimensional perspective cannot be offered as an expression of the world that we perceive and so cannot assume a privileged conformity with the object. This observation obliges us to reconsider the child's drawing. For now we no longer have the right or any need to define the child's drawing solely in relation to the final stage at which it rejoins two-dimensional perspective. Luquet describes the following stages in this progression: fortuitous realism, abortive realism, intellectual

1. TRANSLATOR: Although there is no such chapter as the text now stands, the relationship between thought and expression is clearly considered throughout.

realism, and, finally, visual realism.[2] But as we have seen, two-dimensional perspective is not a form of realism. It is a construction. To understand the stages preceding it, we must not speak of *inattentiveness* or *synthetic incapacity* as if perspectival drawing were already there before the child's eyes, and the whole problem were to explain why he was not motivated by it. On the contrary, we should try to understand the primordial modes of expression for their own sake and as positive accomplishments. One is obliged to represent a cube by a square and two lozenges adjoining one of its sides and its base only *if* one has decided to project the spectacle on paper. In other words, it follows only if one constructs a relief in which there figures, along with the object, the base on which it stands, nearby objects with their respective orientations in the vertical and horizontal planes and their scale in depth, so that the numerical values of these different relations can be recovered and read according to a single scale—in short, where one could gather a maximum of *information* not so much on the spectacle as on the invariants that are recoverable in the perception of any spectator from any point of view whatsoever.

In a way paradoxical only in appearance, two-dimensional perspective is adopted from a certain point of view in order to achieve a notation of the world that would be valid for everyone. It congeals the lived perspective and, in order to represent what is perceived, adopts an index of deformation which is characteristic of my standpoint. Yet by this very artifice, two-dimensional perspective constructs an image that is immediately translatable into the optics of any other point of view and, in this sense, in an image of the world as it is or a configuration of every possible perspective. It gives subjectivity an axiomatic satisfaction through the deformation which it introduces into appearances. But since this deformation is systematic and occurs according to the same index in every part of the scene, it transports me amidst the very things and shows them to me as God sees them. Rather, to be more precise, two-dimensional perspective does not give me a human view of the world. It gives me *knowledge that can be*

2. G. H. Luquet, *Le Dessin enfantin* (Paris: Alcan, 1927).

obtained from a human viewpoint by a god who does not get caught in finitude. Such a view is a goal which one may seek in the expression of the world. But one could have another intention.

We could try not to render our relation to the world, in accordance with what it is under the gaze of an infinite intelligence. Then, at a stroke, the canonical, normal, or "true" type of expression would no longer be two-dimensional perspective. We would then be liberated from the constraints that perspective imposed upon drawing—free, for example, to express a cube by six squares "disjointed" and juxtaposed on the paper, free to draw in the two faces of a bobbin and join them by a sort of bent stovepipe, to represent death by transparency in its coffin or the look by two eyes separated from the head, free not to have to mark the "objective" contours of the alley or of the face and in contrast to indicate the cheeks by a circle. This is what the child does. It is also what Claude Lorrain does when he renders the presence of light through the shadows which surround it and thus more eloquently than he could have rendered it by trying to draw the shafts of light. The point is that the aim is no longer to construct an "objective" emblem of the spectacle or to communicate with whoever looks at the drawing by providing him with the key to the numerical relations true for any and all perceptions of the object. The aim is to leave on the paper a trace of our contact with this object and this spectacle, insofar as they made our gaze and virtually our touch, our ears, our feeling of risk or of destiny or of freedom vibrate. It is a question of leaving a testimony and not any more of providing information. The drawing is no longer to be *read* the way it was until recently. It is not to be dominated by the look. We are no longer to find in it the pleasure of embracing the world. The drawing is to be received. It will concern us like some decisive word. It will arouse in us the profound schema which has settled us in our body and through the body in the world. It will bear the mark of our finitude and thereby, and by means of that very finitude, it will lead us to the secret substance of the object of which previously we possessed only the envelope.

Two-dimensional perspective gave us the finitude of our perception, projected and flattened out, until it had become *prose* under the gaze of a god. The child's ways of expression, once they have been deliberately recaptured by an artist in a genuinely creative gesture, will, on the contrary, yield us the secret resonance through which our finitude opens up to the being of the world and becomes poetry. We should also have to say about the expression of time what we were just saying about spatial expression. The child's "graphic narrations" combine the successive scenes of a story into a single picture, drawing in the invariable elements of the scenery only once, or even drawing in just once each of the characters taken in an attitude suited to a given moment in the story. Thus the child is the sole hearer of the entire story at the time considered, and all the scenes communicate through the thickness of time, staking out the story further and further on. To the eye of the "reasonable" adult, who conceives time as a series of juxtaposed temporal points, such a narrative would be likely to seem broken and obscure. But if we follow time as we live it, the present still touches and still holds the past in its hand.

The present is in a strange coexistence with the past, and only the ellipses in graphic narration can express this movement of the story which encroaches its present onto its future in the way the "fold" expresses the coexistence of the invisible and visible aspects of the object or the secret presence of the object in the piece of furniture where it has been put away. There is indeed quite a difference between the child's involuntary drawing, the residue of an undivided experience, even taken with plastic gestures, false drawing (like false writing or the false talking of babble) and the authentic expression of appearances which is not content to exploit the ready-made world of the body and add to it the world of a principle of systematic expression. But objectivity symbolizes what is in front the same way as what is above, whereas the child's drawing situates "objective" drawing in a series of expressive operations which seek, without any guarantee, to recover the being of the world and to make us perceive objective drawing as a particular example of that endeavor.

There is never any question of knowing whether or not a painter uses two-dimensional perspective. It is a matter of knowing whether he perceives two-dimensional perspective as an infallible recipe for his work—then he forgets his task and is no painter—or whether he comes across it in the course of an expressive exercise with which it appears compatible or even plays the role of a useful aid but never gives the whole sense of that effort. Cézanne abandons two-dimensional perspective for a whole period of his career because he seeks expression through color. The expressive richness of an apple makes him edge over its contours and he cannot be content with the space they prescribe for him. Another painter—or Cézanne himself, in his last period—observes the "laws" of perspective or, rather, has no need to set them aside because he is seeking expression through the sketch and no longer needs to fill his canvas.

The important thing is that, even when it is there, perspective should be present only the way the rules of grammar are present in a style. The objects in a modern painting "bleed," their substance spreads under our eyes, they directly question our gaze, and they test the pact of coexistence that we have made with the world by means of our whole body. The objects in a classical painting have a more discreet way of speaking to us. Sometimes it is an arabesque, a scarcely materialized trace of the brush, that appeals to our incarnation, while the rest of the language at a decent distance, in the fullness of time, or in the eternal, and abandons itself to the proprieties of two-dimensional perspective. The essential thing is that, in the one case as in the other, the universality of the painting is never the result of the numerical relationships which may obtain in it. The communication between the painter and us is not founded upon a prosaic objectivity, and the constellation of signs always guides us toward a signification that was nowhere prior to itself.

But these remarks apply to language.

Index